Copyright © 2020 by Torre L. Walls

For permission requests, write to the publisher, addressed "Attention: Permissions Coordinator," at the address below.
Jai Publishing House Incorporated
1230 Peachtree Street NE, 19th Floor
Atlanta, Georgia 30309
www.jaipublishing.com

Cover art by Chrissi Knighton Burrell, www.thedesignbrand.com

Printed in the United States of America

ISBN: 978-1-7352082-9-9

This devotional belongs to

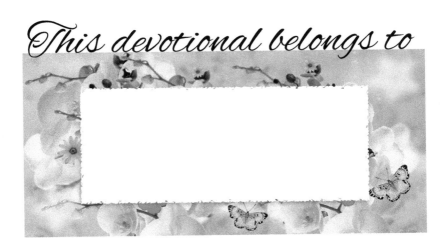

Dedication

Glory to God in the Highest for the Great
Things He has Done!

To Shannon, Morgan and Ambrosia, I love
you all so much!

Here's to Living Your Lives with
Authenticity!

~ Table of Contents ~

Foreword

My first introduction to Torre L. Walls was via her daughters, Morgan and Ambrosia. I have spent the last thirty years of my life coaching and uplifting youth and women, and have had the honor of coaching clients in 13 countries and 44 states in the United States of America.

I met whom I called the "Walls girls" as I coordinated the Summer Youth Empowerment Program in Danville, Illinois and was extremely impressed by their tenacity, leadership, intelligence and work ethic. I was later to find out that they were Torre's daughters. Always intrigued by what allows some kids to thrive while others in similar circumstances crash and burn, I watched Ms. Walls from afar and eventually got to know her father, a local businessman who made the best ribs I've ever had.

Torre's quiet demeanor may fool some, but when I met her, there was no doubt in my mind of the power and anointing on her life, whether she was ready to acknowledge and fully step into it or not. A few years later, I moved from Danville, but I kept in touch with her daughters and celebrated their accomplishments and successes. And through them, I got even more insight into the foundation their mother had laid for them and her fierce determination.

Years later, I was in Danville for a book signing and held an intimate gathering for women—which Torre, her mother and daughter attended. Torre did not speak much, but I sensed plenty from her. That night, as I reminisced on our time together, I wrote these words about her: "Still waters run deep."

I remember praying for her and the other ladies in the gathering, that God would reveal the purpose for each of their lives and give them the courage to boldly live it out.

When Torre reached out to me many, many months later, it was with amazement, a deep sense of gratitude and excitement that I listened to the dreams God had stirred up in her. Her decision to say YES, to throw off her doubts, and to fully embrace the vision she had been given was exhilarating.

The Bible says that out of the comfort we have received, we will comfort others. I knew that Torre was uniquely equipped to help hurting, broken, disillusioned women find their way back to wholeness, joy and purpose. But even with all she had shared, and all God had revealed to me, I must admit I still had a limited understanding of the depth of the power, insight, strength and wisdom she possesses.

We agreed to work together for twelve weeks, during which time I would coach her to write and publish her first of many devotionals and books, and to launch the initiative God had given her, Foundational Rainbows. While a great percentage of my clients who wanted to become authors have done just that, there are still some who struggle with the discipline and confidence it takes to hear from God and write from a place of authenticity, vulnerability and power.

I hoped for the best for Torre, but only she could do the work necessary to birth the vision with which she had been entrusted. Torre initially assumed that it would take her six months to complete her first devotional. I challenged her on the timeline, and we scaled it back to a mere 10 weeks.

Sisters, what if I told you that Torre went to work with an intensity I rarely see and actually completed the manuscript for the devotional you now hold in your hands in two months!!! In one of the devotionals, she writes, "Know your limits, but do not fear your limitations." This must have been the mindset she employed while homeschooling her granddaughter during the day, in the midst of COVID-19 pandemic, and writing at night. Each time on our weekly accountability sessions, I would be blown away by her steadfastness, her focus, and her ability to apply the Word of God in overcoming all the challenges and setbacks. She never wavered in her obedience to the vision.

Today, you hold in your hands a devotional written just for you, Authenticity: Woes to Wisdom 30-Day Devotional (Volume 1) by Torre L. Walls. This Devotional is everything you have been praying for to take you from a place of uncertainty, hurt, disillusionment to boldly living out your purpose with joy.

Committing to this 30-Day Devotional will undoubtedly change your life for the better as it has changed mine. Using relatable stories and experiences from her life and the lives of others, Torre has given us a devotional that will transform our quiet time with God, even as it heals and propels you to unearth your buried dreams and aspirations.

This is NOT your average devotional. In Authenticity: Woes to Wisdom (Volume 1), Torre exhorts and supports women through their healing with Scripture, Inspiration, Songs of praise and worship, and, last but not least, Prayer to ultimately gain wisdom of their Godly purposed potential. Torre shares her traumas, domestically and sexually, as she delivers a message for any woman who has ever felt like "Nobody" and she guides and shows them how to go from feeling and living like a nobody to become NoBoDy (New-found Original Blessing Other Destiny-Bound Yearnings).

Her layered approach to teaching the Word of God and encouraging women for true transformation will have you not just meditating on scripture, applying scripture to your life as she shares her stories, but also singing and dancing in the Spirit and knowing exactly how to pray through your circumstances.

This is the full teaching and worshipping experience you need to break off those physical, emotional, and spiritual chains and soar high as you step into your purpose. I have no doubt that this devotional will transform your life.

Aya Fubara Eneli, Esq.

Life Coach, Inspirational Speaker, Attorney and Best-selling Author of Live Your Abundant Life and Reclaim Your Life: Guidance for Wives at the Crossroads

www.ayaeneli.com

Approved

> **2 Timothy 2:15 (NIV)**
>
> Do your best to present yourself to God as one approved, a worker who does not need to be ashamed and who correctly handles the word of truth.

My First Level

Thirty-four years of church service. I served and worked as the administrative assistant; served on the usher ministry; attended and taught Sunday school; sang in the choir for special programs; I did not attend bible study.

Although I typed the Pastor's sermons, I did not study the content for my own spiritual nourishment. Working in God's Kingdom was my assignment for this time period. I acclimated myself to being a worker for the Lord and unknowingly I was seeking God's stamp of approval through works and not by studying His Word.

Oh, my, my, my!! It is a good thing my Father in heaven looks at the heart. 1 Samuel 16:7 (MSG) says:

But God told Samuel, "Looks aren't everything. Don't be impressed with his looks and stature. I've already eliminated him. God judges persons differently than humans do. Men and women look at the face; God looks into the heart."

My Second Level

Fifteen years of service with awesome teaching and preaching. I Served as the administrative assistant for two different dynamic pastors; coordinated the praise dance ministry; taught Sunday school for preschoolers; sang in the choir for the Women's day program only; taught seasoned saints praise dances; attended Sunday school and bible study.

I developed a desire to serve, minister, praise, worship and work for God with all that is in me! I sought to have a relationship with Him. I longed to have the Holy Spirit to enlighten my mind, body and soul as I delved deeply into studying His Word.

My Third Level

Two years of growth, knowledge, wisdom and service. Before I moved to Texas, I was attending a church where the man of God biblically taught with such specificity, knowledge and wisdom. I attended Sunday School with a great bunch of Christian ladies. The women's ministry had an outreach ministry partnering with the local women's crisis center and their families.

We worked diligently in God's Kingdom eagerly seeking His approval. We grew as a ministry even more in Him! Glory to God! 2 Peter 3:18 (NKJV) says:

> …but grow in the grace and knowledge of our Lord and Savior Jesus Christ. To Him be the glory both now and forever! Amen

My Fourth Level

I have reached another spiritual level with my Father in my move to Texas. I am attending church in Texas where I worship God with both my grown daughters every Sunday. The Pastor is an anointed vessel being used by the Lord in extraordinary ways. He is a fervent teacher and preacher of God's Holy Word. The church members are on fire for the Lord! I am on fire for the Lord!

I am Your vessel, use me Lord!

Isaiah 6:8 (NLT) says:

> *Then I heard the Lord asking, "Whom should I send as a messenger to this people? Who will go for us?" I said, "Here I am. Send me."*

The Next Level For Me

To be determined… Glory to God!

Moment of Truth	Song
Visitor ˅ Validation ˅ Valued ˅ VICTORIOUS	Lead Me, Guide Me by Velma Willis
PRAYER	

Dear Father, Thank You for leading and directing my path. Thank You for when I was growing, You kept me and loved me enough to align me with the plans You have for my life. In Jesus' Name I Pray, Amen

Barriers

> ### Proverbs 3:5-6 (KJV)
>
> Trust in the Lord with all thine heart; and lean not unto thine own understanding. In all thy ways acknowledge Him, and He shall direct thy paths.

Detoured

As a teen mom in high school, I was considered a community statistic. I was ridiculed, mocked and teased. Being a teen mom was my societal pit. I did not fit in anywhere. I was in a wilderness created from my own youthful decisions.

I persevered through all the noise and ridicule. I moved on to graduate high school in December; gave birth to my son in February the following year; and walked the stage with my graduating class later in May. 2 Chronicles 15:7 (NIV) says:

But as for you, be strong and do not give up, for your work will be rewarded.

Do not be defined by your mistakes! Own them and keep moving forward.

Strange Land

The month of August became full. I began attending a community college and gained employment with five different employers to support my son (college work-study, major department store, key drug store, a factory front office position and the local newspaper).

I began my college quest majoring in computer science. There were no instructors who looked like me. There was no fit for me academically or socially. I did not believe in myself enough to complete the program. I ultimately became my own barrier. I fought a good fight, only to give up.

The counselor later steered me to begin a new program in the secretarial field. I was told this area would be a better fit for me. I finally completed my Associate in Applied Science in Data Processing/Office Personnel; and I was grateful. I allowed barriers to ensue because again, there were no instructors who looked like me. Not to mention, there were very few students who resembled me in the classrooms.

Stereotypes resulted as some staff and other students did not see me staying in the program, once I received the financial aid refund. I was not seen as the hardworking, committed and dedicated student I knew I was. They did not know who fueled my desire to succeed. It was my son. I wanted to make him proud of me. Of course, once the instructors recognized I was goal-oriented and committed to seeing this program through, I was accepted and treated with the respect I had earned.

Although I did not know it during my early college years, my first degree would be a foundationally-sound beginning for all areas of my life. I have excellent skills that manifested from those top-notch administrative tools.

Matthew 21:22 (KJV) says:

And all things, whatsoever ye shall ask in prayer, believing, ye shall receive.

Believe it; Receive it!

The Revelation

I later enlisted in the United States Army. After my active duty tours were over, I returned home, served in the Army Reserves, and took advantage of the Post-9/11 GI Bill program — for service members discharged after September 10, 2001 to receive college tuition assistance.

While raising my family, I became a career community college student. I was happily and aimlessly taking class, after class, after class while working full- and part-time jobs.

I had earned enough credits at the community college level to have obtained a Bachelor's degree. I wandered around for many years taking a class here and a class there with no direction. I took general classes that interested me.

One day I attended a higher learning college fair on campus and strolled over to one of the information booths. They absolutely blew my mind with material. I had no earthly idea I could, or even would, obtain a Bachelors of Science degree. This degree program was geared toward the working student. Once my community college credits were transferred, I had only a couple of classes to complete before I began core courses.

I loved going to college so much I continued my academic journey by attaining a Master's degree in technology, and completing a certificate program, too.

In 2007, a family film called "Meet the Robinson's" premiered. The main character of the story had a saying to "keep moving forward." Galatians 6:9 (NIV) says:

Let us not become weary in doing good, for at the proper time we will reap a harvest if we do not give up.

No matter the barriers, obstacles, differences, set-up or setbacks, remember to **KEEP MOVING FORWARD**!

Moment of Truth	Song
You are a torch! No more flickering! Stay lit! Now lead!	We Fall Down by Donnie McClurkin

PRAYER

Dear Lord, Thank You for keeping me even when I was knowingly doing wrong and when I did not know I was doing wrong. Thank You for never giving up on me even when I stumbled and fell. Thank You Father for ordering my steps. As You continue to lead me and guide me Lord, I will forever bless Your precious name and give You all the glory, honor and praise You are ever so worthy of. In Jesus' Name I pray, Amen

Green Light

---

2 Corinthians 5:17 (KJV)

Therefore if any man be in Christ, he is a new creature: old things are passed away; behold, all things are become new.

Appointed

My Pastor decided he wanted a new ministry at the church. He announced to me he wanted to add a praise dance ministry to the church, and he wanted me to oversee it.

"What was he thinking?" I thought.

My immediate response was no; not me! I did not feel I deserved to be in charge of anyone's ministry. He told me to think about it, yet, I didn't feel qualified to lead the youth of this church. I was a freshly divorced mother now with three children; one son and two daughters. I was a new member and newly hired as the Administrative Assistant at the church. I settled in my mind the Pastor had asked the wrong person to lead this ministry.

Although I was a posh choreographer of a local scholarship pageant for young ladies for over 15 years, in my mind this talent was considered secular and would not transfer to being able to lead a church ministry.

I sought advice from my sister-in-law who grew up in this church. I trusted her counsel as she urged, "Do it!" With the self-imposed pressure of "not being able" to do it alone, I asked my sister-in-law to be my partner, and she agreed.

I went to the Pastor and told him I would do it if my sister-in-law could partner with me. He asked me why and I gave him excuse after excuse. He finally agreed to both my sister-in-law and I being the leadership of the praise dance ministry, Shekinah.

We worked hard coming up with our first two praise dances. The youth were eager and ready to learn and minister. I read up on the rules, regulations and protocols of a praise dance ministry and went to a couple of workshops around the area. I was trying to equip myself with all the knowledge to do the Lord's work.

Teaching Godly Direction… Proverbs 3:5-6 (NLT) says:

> *Trust in the Lord with all your heart; do not depend on your own understanding. Seek His will in all you do, and He will show you which path to take.*

Equipped...

The Shekinah Praise Dance Ministry was truly a ministry anointed by God. He directed our steps. The ministry was powerful! The praise dances were so uplifting and true to His essence that even the biggest skeptic of 'dance' in the church had been converted. In the beginning, my sister-in-law and I taught the praise dances. Later, it shifted to only me, as many of the praise dance members now wanted to minister and choreograph praise dances. What the Father had birthed in this ministry had transferred to His youth.

If The Shekinah Praise Dance Ministry veered off course, the Lord's presence corrected me in this area of His ministry. I started noticing Shekinah moving in a slothful direction. I did not understand what was going on. I shared the experience with the

Pastor, and he told me the atmosphere was not favorable to a Godly ministry. Shekinah did not perform, Shekinah ministered; period. I had to learn not to reduce Him to mere performances.

The Lord provided me with the fortitude to teach the members of this ministry. This meant I had to be the leader that prepared the members for ministry by providing the praise dance music, lyrics and dance attire appropriate for all ages. I had to be timely and present. I had to show up.

When God calls you to lead, do not look at yourself as others would view you; see yourself the way God sees you. He will provide you with everything you need to succeed in His Name!

He has given you the green light; now teach. Matthew 28:19-20 (NIV) says:

> *Therefore go and make disciples of all nations, baptizing them in the name of the Father and of the Son and of the Holy Spirit, 20 and teaching them to obey everything I have commanded you. And surely I am with you always, to the very end of the age.*

Released

I am a behind-the-scenes type person. I will work my butt off if you just let me be the me I think I should be. The Lord has a way of drawing out those talents and gifts He has placed in us. I was more than prepared to lead the Shekinah Praise Dance Ministry. In the beginning, I took on the same mindset as Moses. God asked him to lead His people; Moses was reluctant and later said he would if his brother Aaron could go with him to confront Pharaoh. Because of Moses' stutter, he felt he was not able to lead God's people; he felt he could not speak on their behalf, because he had a speech impediment (refer to Exodus 4:10-16).

My Father uses the most ordinary people to do extraordinary things.

Move beyond your comfort zone. Deuteronomy 31:6 (NIV) says:

Be strong and courageous. Do not be afraid or terrified because of them, for the Lord your God goes with you; he will never leave you nor forsake you.

Moment of Truth	Song
Know Him; Grow in Him; Flow with Him; Show up with Him!	Best For Last by Donald Lawrence, featuring Yolanda Adams

PRAYER

Lord, O precious Lord! I come to You with a bowed head and a humble heart. Thank You for loving me right where I am! Thank You for allowing me to grow in my relationship with You. You chose me to lead Your ministry and I will be forever grateful for Your trust in me. Thank You for not giving up on me. In Jesus' Name I pray, Amen

Humility

> Proverbs 15:33 (NIV)
>
> Wisdom's instruction is to fear the Lord, and humility comes before honor.

Humiliate

 was employed by 5 community places for over 2 years; albeit 2 were seasonal positions.

A military recruiter's sole purpose is to get you to sign up to be a soldier in their prospective military service, no matter what. They tell you what you want to hear. They slick up their word usage to make it all sound legitimate. Their bottom line is all that is running through their minds.

My bottom line was, I just wanted to make a better life for my son. The idea of leaving him terrified me. When I signed over guardianship to my parents, I made sure the language basically stated I could have my son back when I wanted him. I was leery about the attorney and possible slippery slope verbiage.

As leery as I was about the attorney, why did I not apply that to the recruiter. I trusted him when he said, "Absolutely, you will be able to send for your son once you get to your first duty station." That turned out to be a lie. "Will my first duty station be stateside?" I asked the recruiter. "Yes," he said, "They rarely ship soldiers overseas fresh out of Advanced Individual Training (AIT)." I later found out that he lied, again.

Sign me up Mr. Recruiter, but first, see me for who I am. Philippians 2:3 (NIV) says:

Do nothing out of selfish ambition or vain conceit. Rather, in humility value others above yourselves...

Humiliated

I humiliated myself by not asking the right questions. I humiliated myself because I had one goal in mind and that was to raise my son and be able to do so financially. I messed up. I was 21 years old; I had a degree; I was smart, right? I did not have a clue that my world was headed for some rough stuff.

I endured basic training in a cold climate. I embraced AIT to learn my Military Occupational Specialties (MOS) in a warmer climate.

Learn and relearn. Proverbs 11:2 (NLT) says:

Pride leads to disgrace, but with humility comes wisdom.

Humiliation

My first duty station was overseas. I worked hard and I followed orders. I told my Sergeant I was ready to ask leadership for permission to allow my son to come live with me.

Army leadership replied. Pass the upcoming room inspection, then we will decide. Passed inspection. Well, attain promotional status to your next rank of Specialist 4/E-4; when I enlisted, I was ready and I already had an educational degree which allowed me to begin my enlistment as a PFC/E-3. I attained my E-4 rank.

I was living in the barracks. I went back to leadership to let him know I completed the tasks he had commanded. "Now, may I send for my son?"

Leadership told me there is one more thing I needed to do for him. I said, "Yes, Sir?" Leadership sat behind a massive desk and began unbuckling his pants. Leadership then told me to 'TOP HIM OFF'—explaining oral sex was not sex and that I could never prove what he was doing to me because it was not physical sexual intercourse. I can still smell leadership's disgusting smell. This manipulation, degradation and exploitation went on for months.

Leadership would tell the runner (person on guard duty at the barracks) late at night, to run up and get me from my room. I can still hear those footsteps as they got louder and louder until he reached my third-floor door and then tap, tap, tap, "Top wants to see you." I was always on point, never knowing when I would be summoned. As time had passed, leadership eventually told me he would leave me alone if I was married.

So, guess what, I got married to my 'homeboy', moved off base and leadership left me alone and eventually left for another duty station. I was able to get my son, but the cost is an ongoing psychological battle still with me today.

I still live with my involuntary senses because of leadership's intentional choice. Romans 8:35-39 (NIV) says:

[35] Who shall separate us from the love of Christ? Shall trouble or hardship or persecution or famine or nakedness or danger or sword? [36] As it is written: "For your sake we face death all day long; we are considered as sheep to be slaughtered. [37] No, in all these things we are more than conquerors through him who loved us. [38] For I am convinced that neither death nor life, neither angels nor demons, neither the present nor the future, nor any powers, [39] neither height nor depth, nor anything else in all creation, will be able to separate us from the love of God that is in Christ Jesus our Lord.

Humiliating

Cause: humiliating my 'homeboy' by marrying him for all the wrong reasons.

Effect: I felt I deserved the attempts on my life, the verbal, physical and mental abuse.

Humility

Yes, I had a son. Yes, I lacked sexual knowledge tremendously. Yes, I blame myself. I was not ready for the wickedness of this world! I just wanted to provide a good life for my son. I just wanted to be a good Mommie.

- All leadership remind me of a 'top' situation.

- I held myself in low regard.

- I internalized everything.

- Lived in my own mental hell jail.

- I did not make waves; I tried to be the woman of obedience.

- I avoided confrontation.

- I had to say enough was enough, leave the judgment of the heart in God's hands.

- The ordeals led me to humble myself.

- I tried to hide, cover up and silence my military sexual trauma (MST).

- I busied myself with others.

- I hoped they would never see what 'top' did to me. In my mind I felt others could see my 'Scarlet Letter'

- I put my head down and put my hand to the plow!

- ▷ I became a force for God!

- ▷ I raised my 3 children. I kept each of them engaged in activities for their good and later realized I used it for my good.

- ▷ I filled my days with helping, serving, teaching, and guiding.

In spite of… I am Truly Blessed! Jeremiah 17:8 (NKJV) says:

For he shall be like a tree planted by the waters, Which spreads out its roots by the river, And will not [a]fear when heat comes; But its leaf will be green, And will not be anxious in the year of drought, Nor will cease from yielding fruit.

Moment of Truth	Song
"Humility is not thinking less of yourself, it is thinking of yourself less." -CS LEWIS	Let go Let God by P J Morton featuring The Walls Group
PRAYER	

Heavenly Father, please allow me to forgive Leadership for trauma endured in my life. Lord, give me the relief to heal myself for the naïve mistakes of my past. Dear Father, Thank You for keeping me even when danger was lurking mightily near. Thank You Lord for using me as I continue to move forward in Your precious Son's Name, Amen

Imagine

> ### Philippians 3:13-14 (NIV)
>
> Brothers and sisters, I do not consider myself yet to have taken hold of it. But one thing I do: Forgetting what is behind and straining toward what is ahead, I press on toward the goal to win the prize for which God has called me heavenward in Christ Jesus.

Imagine This

I suffer from Post Traumatic Stress Disorder - Military Sexual Assault (PTSD – MST), anxiousness and depression. I now know my Father had a plan for me. He has used me in the past to teach young women the art of dance that required grace and elegance. He anointed a ministry that allowed me to lead and guide young women to praise Him through dance. Now He is holding me close as I write devotionals empowering and encouraging women. He wants me to share my journey with you. I desire to help anyone to overcome their deepest and darkest.

He is allowing me to reach out to you to help me help you. I have tried therapy, but for me, the therapist would use cookie-cutter processes and not touch on the uniqueness of my trauma. Imagine, if He can use me all broken, and yet, I am still coloring; then guess what my friend, He can do the same for you!

God will meet you right where you are. Let Him guide you to a complete and limitless life in Him. Psalms 34:4-8 (MSG) says:

[4] God met me more than halfway, he freed me from my anxious fears. [5] Look at him; give him your warmest smile. Never hide your feelings from him. [6] When I was desperate, I called out, and God got me out of a tight spot. [7] God's angel sets up a circle of protection around us while we pray. [8] Open your mouth and taste, open your eyes and see—how good God is. Blessed are you who run to him.

Imagine That

Imagine a life that is changed to a new way of thinking about living, such as worldly ideals, mind-shifts, and biases. Old opinions are replaced with new thoughts that align with God's purpose for your life.

This is not an overnight process it progresses over time by growing in your relationship with God. Studying His Word, daily! Praying to Him. Having little conversations with Him throughout the day. Just a little talk with Jesus will do ya.

Ask for God's perfect wisdom in every decision you make no matter how small, and commit yourself to His Holy Word.

Knowing God's Will for your life will give you peace that surpasses all understanding. Philippians 4:7 (NIV) says:

And the peace of God, which transcends all understanding, will guard your hearts and your minds in Christ Jesus.

Imagine to Infinity and Beyond......

Imagine more!

There is more for you; much more!

Some of us are sitting on buried power of divine potential with your purpose waiting to be tapped into!

Once released, it will manifest itself bubbling over like a shaken can of soda... wooosshhh!

Ephesians 3:20 (NKJV) says:

Now to him who is able to do exceedingly abundantly above all that we ask or think (imagine), according to the (His) power that work in us, (emphasis: mine)

Moment of Truth	Song
Just Imagine…!	Imagine Me by Kirk Franklin I Can Only Imagine by MercyMe

PRAYER
Lord, You knew me in my mother's womb. You molded me and prepped me for this very moment. In my finite mind, I could never imagine; but because You are Infinite, You know me. Thank You for giving me peace in weary places in my life. Sometimes this world can make me feel like a nobody, but I am thankful You know me as Your friend and Your child! Father, I know that You love me. I rest today Lord in the strength of Your loving arms. Praise God! In Jesus' Name, Amen

Day 6

Rainbow

Genesis 9:12 (NIV)

And God said, "This is the sign of the covenant I am making between me and you and every living creature with you, a covenant for all generations to come...

Rain

How many will admit that when you see a rainbow your first thought was the possibility of a pot of gold at the end of it? Raise your hand or just chuckle to yourself.

I believe rainbows are a majestic sight to see.

Realistically, there would be no rainbows without rain and sunshine. We must endure the rain to enjoy a rainbow.

To encounter a Rainbow, you must go through and weather the storms.

Rainbows motivate us to remain steadfast in the course of dark times. Genesis 9:13 (NLT) says:

I have placed my rainbow in the clouds. It is the sign of my covenant with you and with all the earth.

Arch

Rainbows are magical!

Scientifically, rainbows are pretty darn splendiferous. They use descriptors like wavelength, spectrum, reflects, refracts and disperses. All that takes away from how wondrous it is to just look at the rainbow's magnificence.

When trouble and trials arise, we need to trust and hold on to God's promises.

Because of His Covenant, when things get tough, rainbows remind us to trust in God's promises and faithfulness. Romans 8:28 (NLT) says:

And we know that God causes everything to work together[a] for the good of those who love God and are called according to his purpose for them.

Hebrews 10:23 (NIV) says:

Let us hold unswervingly to the hope we profess, for he who promised is faithful.

Light

Rainbows are a covenant from God. Rainbows remind us of God's abundant grace and mercy. No matter how much I love a rainbow, it fades in comparison when we think about how Jesus was the propitiation for our sins. Joshua 1:9 (NIV) says:

Have I not commanded you? Be strong and courageous. Do not be afraid; do not be discouraged, for the Lord your God will be with you wherever you go.

The promise of God's presence is more than enough to sustain us and keep us grounded in His Word and to continually pray in His Son's Name.

Ezekiel 1:28 (NKJV) says:

Like the appearance of a rainbow in a cloud on a rainy day, so was the appearance of the brightness all around it. This was the appearance of the likeness of the glory of the Lord.

Moment of Truth	Song
"Never be afraid to trust an unknown future to a known God." –Corrie Ten Boom	I'LL Trust You by James Fortune I Need Your Glory by James Fortune & FIYA

PRAYER

I trust You Lord with all of me. I trust You to use me as Your vessel of goodness on this earth. I trust Your conviction when I have done wrong. I love You and will forever praise Your name Father! In Jesus' Name, Amen

DAY 7

Uncertain

> ### Psalms 18:2 (NLT)
>
> The Lord is my rock, my fortress, and my savior; my God is my rock, in whom I find protection. He is my shield, the power that saves me, and my place of safety.

The Shift

 MAY 1982

I was 16 years old and had just completed my junior year of high school. I was sick. I was tired. I had the flu. Yeah, that's what's going on with my body… the flu.

I went to the doctor. He informed me that I was pregnant. With all sincerity, I said, "How did this happen?"

He replied, "You know how this happened." The doctor had jokey jokes at a time my mind was completely blown. My world as I knew it came crashing down because I was hot in da pants. My body was preparing to have a whole baby at 16 years old.

I felt as if I had walked around my neighborhood for days in shock trying to decide how I was going to tell my parents. I was overwhelmed with shame. I knew my dad was gonna have a hissy fit all upside my head.

I finally made it home with what seemed like an eternity since I was given the news of my pregnancy. I told my mom first, of course, I had not lost all my marbles just yet. Her immediate response was 'what others might think'. I went upstairs to my room while my mom told my dad. He came upstairs, I braced for what I knew was coming, never knowing – hey I am pregnant he couldn't hit me — nope that scenario never crossed my mind. My dad had on his serious face and he pointed at me and said, "You are going to have this baby" and he descended back down the stairwell.

I had no idea what I wanted. I was Uncertain. Isaiah 41:10 (NIV) says:

> *So do not fear, for I am with you; do not be dismayed; for I am your God. I will strengthen you and help you; I will uphold you with my righteous right hand.*

Physical Release

 OCTOBER 1982

I returned to high school in the fall to begin my senior year.

I had made the pom's squad the previous school year.

I had made it through the football season undetected with no one noticing I was pregnant.

I was able to perform at the basketball assembly prior to the start of the season.

It finally became evident as I could no longer hide the fact I was pregnant, as the skirt was getting snug around my protruding belly.

I had to tell my poms coach who was also my guidance counselor I was pregnant. She lowered her head in disbelief and sadness. She looked at me with such disappointment. She decided not to kick me off the poms squad. She allowed it to be my decision to leave on my own accord.

I left her office. I sat on the outside steps of my high school staring; looking passed the empty parking lot into space, waiting for my mom to pick me up from my last poms practice.

I was certain that I was uncertain of what I was to do next. Psalms 56:3 (NIV) says:

When I am afraid, I put my trust in you.

Trust

 NOVEMBER 1982

I could no longer fit my clothes.

My mom bought me the best looking most fashionable maternity clothes. She was loving me the best she knew how, but all the maternity clothes did, in my child mind, was scream my indiscretion to the other high school students and my teachers.

The students began to notice my belly getting bigger and put two-and-two together to deduce my ever so present pregnancy. They teased me, snickered at me in class, and called me pregnant related names and other names that indicated I was hot in da pants. I was 'that' girl.

I no longer wanted to face the eyes of disgust, the shaking heads and pious ridicule from teachers and/or classmates.

I had completed all requirements and had enough high school credits to graduate early that December.

I was totally uncertain of what was next for me. Psalms 25:4-5 (NIV) says:

Show me your ways, Lord, teach me your paths. Guide me in your truth and teach me, for you are God my Savior, and my hope is in you all day long.

Walk by Faith

 FEBRUARY 1983

My mom can tell you every precise detail of the night we went to the hospital for the birth of my child.

I had taken a Lamaze class, but honey chile that class did not prepare me for what I was about to endure – real daggone childbirth.

I looked up at my nurse and asked her if this (prep for having a baby) was for practice or for real. She did not mock my naivety because she knew I was a child having a child.

She politely told me, "This is for real." She told me I was in labor ready to deliver the baby.

My handsome baby boy was born!

I was a for real- for real mom at 17 years old.

Uncertain, doubtful, fearful, anxious. I had this whole itty-bitty bundle of precious life in my childlike hands.

For certain everything had changed.

I had to grow up pretty darn quick.

My responsibility level developed quickly.

I had to understand his cries and diapers, diapers, and more diapers.

I was certain I had the best parents in the whole wide world then and now.

Although I maintained full responsibility for my son, my parents loved him, helped take care of him, boasted on him, doted on him and defended me regarding my childish choices. My parents allowed us to live with them. There was never a doubt in their minds my son and I would not live with them. The comments from their peanut gallery friends indicated they would 'never' let their daughter(s) live with them if their daughter(s) had got knocked up.

Certainly, I was going to work really hard to support my son.

Certainly, I was going to get a good education to support my son.

Certainly, I was not going to accept public assistance, no offense to anyone who does, this was just my choice not to.

I was certain I was going to own up to my responsibility.

Certainly, I would proudly graduate at my commencement with my class, May 1983.

Certainly, I would begin community college in August 1983.

What was done was done. I had to forgive myself and continue to move forward.

I worked several jobs, some seasonal and some yearly to support my son.

I was for sure; I was certain, I was gonna be the best daggone mom to my son.

My direction became certain. Isaiah 40:31 (KJV) says:

> But they that wait upon the Lord shall renew their strength; they shall mount up with wings as eagles; they shall run, and not be weary; and they shall walk, and not faint.

Moment of Truth	Song
God gives you the umph to move forward despite uncertainties.	They That Wait by Fred Hammond featuring John P. Kee

PRAYER

Lord, I can be certain that You are a personal Savior who is a promise keeper; You are Jehovah Jireh our Provider; You are Jehovah Shalom, our Lord of Peace; You are Jehovah Rapha, our Healer; You are Jehovah Nissi, Lord of our Victory; You are Immanuel, always with us; You are a patient God; You are a forgiving God! I give You all the glory and the praise. I worship You! I honor You! Glory to Your Name Father! In Jesus' Name I Pray, Amen

Value

> **I Timothy 4:8 (NIV)**
>
> For physical training is of some value, but godliness has value for all things, holding promise for both the present life and the life to come.

Father, Your Love for me is more than I can **Imagine**!

You restored my **Humility** to strengthen my fragility despite my **Uncertainty**.

You **Approved** me, in spite of, all my iniquities.

It was You Lord who calmed the **Waves** and You provided a **Rainbow** after a **Water**-fall.

You gave me the **Green light** to go and take flight with all Your might.

I am glad You revealed in Your Holy Word my **Value,** while You manifested my breakthrough in the midst of my trial.

You let me know in Your Holy Word of my **Value.** Forever I am Grateful! Matthew 6:26 (NIV) says:

> *Look at the birds of the air; they do not sow or reap or store away in barns, and yet your heavenly Father feeds them. Are you not much more valuable than they?*

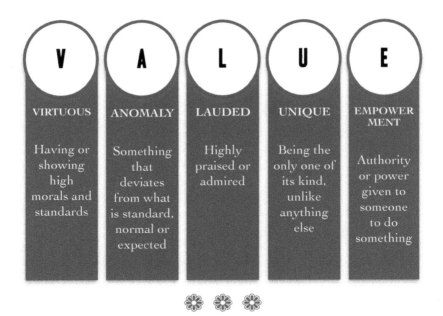

V	**A**	**L**	**U**	**E**
VIRTUOUS	**ANOMALY**	**LAUDED**	**UNIQUE**	**EMPOWER MENT**
Having or showing high morals and standards	Something that deviates from what is standard, normal or expected	Highly praised or admired	Being the only one of its kind, unlike anything else	Authority or power given to someone to do something

Moment of Truth	Song
God is Invaluable!	Worth by Anthony Brown & Group Therapy

PRAYER

Lord, You have brought me a mighty long way! You covered me and protected me when I did not know You as well as I should have. When I look back over my life and I think things over dear heavenly Father I can truly say that I am blessed I have Your testimony on my life. Thank You for spreading your wings and keeping me safe from any hurt, harm or danger. Thank You Father for dispatching Your angels to watch over me daily. In Jesus' Name, Amen

Day 9

Water

> Isaiah 44:3-4 (NIV)
>
> For I will pour water on the thirsty land, and streams on the dry ground; I will pour out My Spirit on your offspring, and My blessing on your descendants. They will spring up like grass in a meadow, like poplar trees by flowing streams.

The Samaritan Woman

All of us have a 'usta do/be' story. I usta do this or that; I usta be this or that. But God…

From 'Love Lifted Me' lyrics…

I was sinking deep in sin,

far from the peaceful shore,

Very deeply stained within,

sinking to rise no more;

But the Master of the sea

heard my despairing cry,

From the waters lifted me,

now safe am I.

Real talk in real time. Imagine this, I was the Samaritan woman who met Jesus at the well and He told me to go and get my husband. I would, like the Samaritan woman tell Him, I do not have a husband. But, Lord have mercy if Jesus called me to the carpet on my immorality and stated how many husbands I have had, girl; I would have been put to shame.

God will expose our iniquities and our wrongdoings. He will put us on full blast y'all!

Jesus approaches the guttermost and the uttermost throughout the bible. He has no favorite woman of God; He loves us equally! He declares time and time again in His Word that He will meet us where we are, but ultimately we have to make that choice to grow in our relationship with Him. We have to be the new creature in Him because we now know Him and we will faithfully and diligently serve Him! Glory!

Romans 3:23 (NKJV) says:

> *...for all have sinned and fall short of the glory of God.*

The Samaritan woman who drank of the living water and was forgiven, cleansed and renewed and was told she would never thirst again.

Isaiah 49:10 (NIV) says:

> *They will neither hunger nor thirst, nor will the desert heat or the sun beat down on them. He who has compassion on them will guide them and lead them beside springs of water.*

What is Living Water?

Living water relates to the presence of God. God is called the source of living water.

Living water is the wisdom of God desiring an intimate relationship with us, which is what the Holy Spirit provides us.

Because the living water comes directly from God, it is strongly linked with God's Spirit in the world. When God promised to redeem His people, He promised to send His Spirit, the Comforter, which is the Holy Ghost! Hallelujah! John 14:26 (KJV) says:

> *But the Comforter, which is the Holy Ghost, whom the Father will send in my name, he shall teach you all things, and bring all things to your remembrance, whatsoever I have said unto you.*

Daily we must recognize and celebrate the grace of God.

We serve a God Who has the grace to handle our minute messes to our extreme entanglements.

The hope is that in the end, He will receive all the glory, honor and praise. John 4:10 (NLT) says:

> *Jesus replied, 'If you only knew the gift God has for you and who you are speaking to, you would ask me, and I would give you living water.'*

How Do I Get This Living Water?

Jesus offered the Samaritan woman to drink from His cup of living water.

After a little talk with Jesus, the Samaritan woman ran back to town to the people of Samaria, the very ones who despised her, to proclaim with unashamed enthusiasm the arrival of the promised Messiah.

God will cause others to look at us differently.

The people of Samaria eagerly responded to Jesus. They, too, yearned for His living water.

Everyone who drinks of the water from the well will be thirsty again, and again, and again, etc. But whoever drinks of the water that He gives, will never thirst again! The water He gives, will become in her a spring of water elevating us to eternal life. John 7:38 (NIV) says:

> *Whoever believes in me, as Scripture has said, rivers of living water will flow from within them.*

How Is Living Water Beneficial?

Jesus Christ forgives our sins, redeems us from our sins and offers us eternal life.

Worldly springs satisfy us temporarily. Immoral springs only make things worse. Sinful springs awaken our thirst instead of quenching it. We will have the desire to constantly want more.

But God! God the Father, God the Son, God the Holy Ghost alone will provide us with His Word which satisfies our utmost spiritual thirsts.

The same Jesus that uses me, can use you too. John 4:24 (KJV) says:

> *God is a Spirit, and those who worship Him must worship Him in spirit and in truth.*

Moment of Truth	Song
Always use your authentic voice to have an authentic conversation with Jesus.	Fall on Me by Shekinah Glory Ministry

PRAYER

Lord, Thank You for being a thirst quencher. Thank You for not picking and choosing Your people and loving us regardless of our faults and failures. I ask You to search me Father and remove whatever is not of You. Please forgive me for sins seen and unseen. Prepare me Father to go into Your world and proclaim Your Worthiness to Your children who are yearning to know You. God, give me the wisdom to discern right from wrong. I accept Your loving conviction when I willfully disobey. In Jesus' Name, Amen

Waves

Psalms 107:29 (NIV)

He stilled the storm to a whisper; the waves of the sea were hushed.

Wipeout Waves

My sister-in-law took on a task I would never do. She packed up my kids, her sisters and their kids, her own kids, and her parents and ventured on a 14-hour road trip to Myrtle Beach, South Carolina. Once they reached their destination, my middle child decided she would venture to the beach, even after she had been warned by her Auntie not go near the water. The waves were dashing high. But my middle child indicated she could swim; so she ran into the water against the wishes of her Auntie. The ominous waves submerged her 50 lb. body almost immediately. My family rushed to her rescue. Thankfully, she was ok.

My middle child, disobediently, but fearlessly rode the wave. Know your limits, but do not fear your limitations. 2 Timothy 1:7 (NKJV) says:

For God has not given us a spirit of fear, but of power and of love and of a sound mind.

Workplace Waves

I applied for a promotional position within an agency I worked for. The director expressed displeasure of how the section was being led by the office manager, my boss, not once, but twice during the eight years I was employed there. The first time, I was the only applicant who applied for the position. The director came into my office and sat down in front of me. He looked up into space, shaking his head and brazenly said, "What was she (me) thinking?"

One year later, the same office manager's status had fallen below expectations. Once again, the position was posted for applicants to apply. Two applied, myself, internally and an external candidate. I made it to the interviewing phase of the process this time. The director decided not to hire anyone and gave me a small monetary token.

Ultimately, in the beginning, I did not let how the director felt deter me from proving this opinion of me wrong. I thought by continuing to work harder, and by being an effective and efficient professional team member, that these efforts would finally be the steps needed to tap into my next level. I believed if I produced a large quantity of quality work, I would be accepted as a burgeoning managerial candidate. I took management and leadership courses to show myself approved.

In the end, despite all my efforts to prove myself, that tempest wave reared its wicked head and it appeared, and I allowed it to whisk me away again—along with all my aspirations, hopes and dreams.

I rode a myriad of waves at this agency. Isaiah 26:3 (NIV) says:

> *You will keep in perfect peace those whose minds are steadfast, because they trust in You.*

Warrior Waves

Have you ever experienced...

- ▷ Being told you look more professional with long hair, when you wear your short hair natural 80% of the time;

- ▷ Someone saying, 'you were only hired for this position because you interviewed well' (this was not a compliment);

- ▷ Receiving all 'does not meet' on your first performance evaluation in a new position;

- ▷ Being humiliated, intimidated and degraded in front of your co-workers and staff?

I can attest to each of these experiences wholeheartedly.

Why did I stay? My reason for staying was a familiar one —I needed my job to support my family. I was a single parent putting my two daughters through school and I had bills to pay.

Believe me ladies, there were plenty of days I wanted to snap back, clap back and rotate my neck back... but God!

I cried myself to sleep many nights asking God to remove this managerial thorn from my side and He showed me — not now my beloved, but soon and very soon. I learned His grace was sufficient during this season.

I learned to put on the full armor of God daily. (Read Ephesians 6:10-18). Each morning, I would fully simulate putting on each piece of His armor and speaking into existence what it biblically represented to me for protection. The most important part of these scriptures was that my manager (flesh and blood) was not the real problem; but how the enemy was using the mind, body and soul of this human vessel to work, weave and wrap his evil ways and darkness validating his sinful nature.

Developing and recognizing this concept alone will save us a lot of grief, sorrow, pain and anger.

Moment of Truth	Song
The waves of life can toss us to and fro. The ebb and flow of life can manifest itself like a rollercoaster ride of eternal waves and loops. (Whispering) Let me tell you something… speak to your rumbling tumbling waves, the power is within you my sister.	I Told The Storm by Greg O'Quinn

PRAYER

Dear Lord, help me to endure the waves of life so that they do not consume me. I know that no one but You can control the waves of life Father. Thank You for allowing me to take solace in knowing You have all power. Lord, sometimes these waves can grow into colossal storms, but this is when I look to the heavens and ask for Your comfort and for You to sustain me in the midst of an attack from the enemy. When the enemy tries to surround me with vessels with intent to harm me, I will continually speak to it and say Father, O my Father forgive them for they know not what they do. Thank you, Father for reminding me that retaliating on my own is not the solution. My reaction on some days may not be pleasing to You, but having a relationship with You will garner conviction from the Holy Spirit which in turn will promote growth in You. In Jesus' Name I pray, Amen

Bread of Life

John 6:35 (NLT)

Jesus replied, "I am the bread of life. Whoever comes to me will never be hungry again. Whoever believes in me will never be thirsty."

One day I was home alone, and a young man came to my door and asked for a drink of water. My human guard went into suspicious mode. I said to him, "Not today."

At the time I did not know it, but as he peered through my screen of my locked door and quoted the latter part of Matthew 25:35 (NIV) to me …*For I was hungry and you gave me something to eat, I was thirsty and you gave me something to drink, I was a stranger and you invited me in.*

When he said this to me, I was still on spiritual milk and was not as vested in the spiritual meat of God's Holy Word. But the conviction and the stirring of my soul conveyed a restlessness within me that did not settle right.

1 Kings 17:12 (NIV) says:

As surely as the Lord your God lives," she replied, "I don't have any bread—only a handful of flour in a jar and a little olive oil in a jug. I am gathering a few sticks to take home and make a meal for myself and my son, that we may eat it—and die."

Now unlike this woman, I had provisions to give this young man, I chose to deny him. God recognizes our need and desire for food. When I reminisce on this memory, I realize my mistake was being judgmental.

There was a couple that would sit in the same place every day and would receive lots of donations during their long day of sitting. I debated a lot about my issue with what I ascertained as their issue. Because in my finite mind, I felt if you can get up everyday and post yourselves on this corner and sit for 4-6 hours, you can get a job. Now remember, this is totally my personal view. But once convicted by the Holy Spirit, I realized in the end it is not my business. It is not for me to question their motive for I serve the Lord and I am to take care of His children on earth. John 6:51 (NLT) says:

> *I am the living bread that came down from heaven. Anyone who eats this bread will live forever; and this bread, which I will offer so the world may live, is my flesh.*

Jesus healed the invalid man at the pool of Bethesda. The lame man was carried and dropped off at the pool daily for the chance to be healed. He told Jesus how he had no one to help him into the pool. Jesus healed this man and the newly healed man reported to religious leadership what Jesus had done for him. He was not thankful for Jesus healing him. (Read John 5 in its entirety)

We are not satisfied spiritually unless we know Jesus; we are not spiritually satisfied unless we have Jesus in our lives; we cannot survive spiritually without Jesus.

Do not think in the physical realm but the spiritual realm. Jesus is essential for life. He is enough; He is essential; He is free to all of those who believe. He is eternal life. Seek after the bread that endures eternal life, which the Son of man will give to you. Jesus is the bread for a hungry soul.

I implore you not to settle for the desires of the world but to partake of the bread of life.

Lord, I will meditate on Your Word. Lord, You are sufficient. Lord, thank You for life eternally. John 6:47-48 (NLT) says:

I tell you the truth, anyone who believes has eternal life. Yes, I am the bread of life!

Moment of Truth	Song
If you bake bread with indifference, you bake a bitter bread that feeds no man's hunger.	You are the Living Word by Fred Hammond & Radical For Christ

PRAYER

God please grant us a deeper understanding and awareness of Your holiness. Lord may we continue to hunger for Your Word and that we are doers and hearers of Your Holy Word. Please remove any obstacles that separate me from being in Your presence Father. Lord I pray for our eyes and ears to be open to Your doctrine and truth. In His Name, Amen

Enemies

Matthew 5:44 (NIV)

But I tell you, love your enemies and pray for those who persecute you...

Enemy

When I was in grade school, segregation of our schools was in the process, and I was a product of being bussed to a previous all White school. Lord have mercy, I remember stepping off that bus and just the uneasiness and the looks of discontentment.

Some days, the adversary would use people of the same race. My parents shopped at Sears and I wore a line of children's clothing called Garanimals; I was teased and picked on because of the way I dressed.

I would go and visit my cousins who lived on the opposite side of town (north end) and we were riding bikes to the local park and kids would ask me, what are you doing out here. They told me I needed to go back to my side of town (east end). All I wanted to do was ride bikes and enjoy the day with my family, but someone looked at me and placed a stigma on me based on where I lived.

Psalms 44:7 (NLT) says:

You are the one who gives us victory over our enemies; you disgrace those who hate us.

Archenemy

I am not a fighter. Never have been, and never will be. But, in middle school, I had just been handed an undeserved detention from my homeroom teacher. I was angry. The bell rang and I stepped out in the hallway, went to my locker, and was approached by this young lady about something she had heard from a mutual friend of ours. I politely said, "Not today."

I proceeded to get my books from my locker, closed the locker and this young lady decided to step in my path. I moved to the other side of the hallway and yet again she stepped in my path again. Well, that was it. I took the books I had in my hand and slammed the books against this young lady's head which knocked her into the lockers, and it took four teachers to get me off of this young lady.

The principal who knew both of my parents, and more importantly he knew me, still had to give me an overnight detention. Should I have been suspended for three days? Yes, but I tried three times to squash whatever this young lady was trying to pursue.

My dad had to leave work to pick me up from school. He did not say a word on the ride home. Once we arrived home, he noticed I had a small scratch right above my lip; so he grabbed the alcohol and cleaned it up. Before he left to go back to work, he asked me if I was ok, to which I responded, "Yes, sir." He closed the door and went back to work. We spoke of it no more.

Psalms 27:2 (NIV) says:

When the wicked advance against me to devour me, it is my enemies and my foes who will stumble and fall.

Haters

Haters are enemies who have sworn that when they look at you, you become the target of what they hate in themselves. I knew growing up I did not fit in. I could tell how people treated me, I just did not fit in.

My son is an old soul and he was liked by many; he fit in. My 9-year-old son came to me one day crying, and I yelled at him not to do that anymore. Sadly, I did not see my son cry again until he was in his late 20's. Ladies, be careful what you say to your children. Proverbs 18:21 (NIV) says:

> *The tongue has the power of life and death, and those who love it will eat its fruit.*

Once during my son's high school years, his sister came home and told me that he was planning to fight this guy at the neighborhood park. I went to the park and I stopped him and made him come home. He was hesitant. He was so mad at me. He later told me as a young adult man that he was teased and ridiculed because I did not let him fight that day. I was a single parent and I made a judgement call to the best of my ability.

My girls did not fit in. I told them not to hit back when a person would come at them sideways. Both were bullied, but my middle child was beaten, bruised, and kicked on several occasions. I can remember three instances when my middle child was involved in fights she did not start. She was struck in the back of her head while walking up the stairs, and once outside a gang of girls commenced to beating on her and her friend, I will call her The Champion. I call this young lady The Champion because she knew how to fight; and she would fight most of the physical fights focused on her and my daughter from girls with mean intent to really hurt them.

You see, my daughter was probably 98 pounds at the time. One instance, she covered the friend and took most of the blows. My daughter should have had broken ribs, ripped out hair, eye socket out... but God! I took her to the doctor and nothing was physically wrong. I took her to the eye doctor, nothing wrong. She just needed to heal from all the bruises. While she protected her friend, God was protecting and shielding her. She would never come to me after these beat downs from inhumane folks. She would go to my parents and they would clean her up lovingly.

My baby never had a fight. She was bullied. I would go to the school and have lunch with her. These bully instances were all in middle school. My baby was short, but she had an athletic body. I would go to the school and speak with the principal and the teachers. But the funny thing is, these bullies in all these instances seemed to go poof. They were not in school anymore. God has a way of removing obstacles for His children. Just remember we are all His children and He will always protect us.

My daughters never disobeyed me about fighting. I knew what their futures were about. I spoke life into them each and every day. I spoke His greatness over their lives knowing my God is a keeper, provider and protector.

Luke 6:35 (NLT) says:

> *Love your enemies! Do good to them. Lend to them without expecting to be repaid. Then your reward from heaven will be very great, and you will truly be acting as children of the Most High, for he is kind to those who are unthankful and wicked.*

Enemy Exposed

Realize the enemy (satan) is using your enemy to try and defeat you. But, John 16:33 (NIV) says:

> *I have told you these things, so that in me you may have peace. In this world you will have trouble. But take heart! I have overcome the world.*

Psalms 23:5 (NLT) says:

You prepare a feast for me in the presence of my enemies. You honor me by anointing my head with oil. My cup overflows with blessings.

1 Peter 5:8 (NKJV) says:

Be sober, be vigilant; because your adversary the devil walks about like a roaring lion, seeking whom he may devour.

Psalms 25:5 (NIV) says:

Guide me in your truth and teach me, for you are God my Savior, and my hope is in you all day long.

Moment of Truth	Song
Ultimate excellence lies not in winning every battle, but in defeating the enemy without ever fighting	Safe in His Arms by Rev. Milton Brunson & The Thompson Community Singers

PRAYER

Lord, when I face unfairness, injustice or abuse, show me how to turn the other cheek and how to help my enemy move closer to You. Heavenly Father, I relinquish all that is in me that is not of You. Give me a clean heart so that I can worship You freely. You are my strength, my strong tower, my protector, my provider. I lift my hands in total praise to You Father. Thank You for all things big and small Lord. In Jesus' Name, Amen

Day 13

Flexible

> ### Philippians 4:12-13 (NLT)
>
> I know how to live on almost nothing or with everything. I have learned the secret of living in every situation, whether it is with a full stomach or empty, with plenty or little. For I can do everything through Christ, who gives me strength.

*F*ather, My focus is on You, Lord! You are the Bread of Life, and Your Word nourishes my body, mind and soul.

I call on You, Father, when I am overwhelmed with sorrow from the rippled effect of my enemies who were used to attack my joy and steal my song of praise.

I remain forever flexible in moving forward receiving Your wonderful will for my life, and I will be cognizant to encourage and uplift Your glorious goodness with others daily.

I will be vigilant, steadfast and unmovable when presenting the good news of the gospel to everyone You place in my path. In my Precious Savior's Name, Amen!

Ephesians 6:10 (NIV) says:

Finally, be strong in the Lord and in His mighty power.

Be Flexible:

Faithful: loyal, constant and steadfast

Loving: feeling or showing love or great care

Eloquent: fluent or persuasive in speaking or writing

Xenas: mighty, strong, confident

Intuitive: using or based on what one feels to be true even without conscious reasoning

Beautifully balanced: pleases the senses or the mind

Ladies: a woman who is refined, polite and well spoken

Excelling Exponentially: surpassing or exceeding more and more rapidly

Romans 12:2 (NIV) says:

Do not conform to the pattern of this world, but be transformed by the renewing of your mind. Then you will be able to test and approve what God's will is — his good, pleasing and perfect will.

Moment of Truth	Song
Favor Flexibility over Inflexibility	Soul's Anthem (It is Well) by Tori Kelly

PRAYER

O, Lord, help me to adapt to the changes that will inevitably come in my life. Teach me to evolve and grow so that I will not become stagnant while waiting to know Your plans for me to work in Your kingdom. I pray for wisdom and knowledge as I pursue to grasp and understand Your precious and Holy Word. Reign down on me Holy Spirit. I invite You to come and dwell in me. Lord, I am ready to meet new challenges that will give You all the glory, honor and praise God. Hallelujah to Your Name! Amen

Focus

Philippians 3:14 (NLT)

I press on to reach the end of the race and receive the heavenly prize for which God, through Christ Jesus, is calling us.

Focus

I am a sports fanatic! It is common knowledge among those who know me, not to interrupt or contact me while Serena Williams was playing tennis. When I am watching Serena play, I am focused on tennis for the duration of the tournament, especially when she makes it to the final. Focusing on Serena's tennis game brings me contentment. Philippians 4:8 (NLT) says:

And now, dear brothers and sisters, one final thing. Fix your thoughts on what is true, and honorable, and right, and pure, and lovely, and admirable. Think about things that are excellent and worthy of praise.

Laser Focused

Serena is laser focused when playing matches at the Grand Slams and some tournaments. She has a mental tunnel vision, athleticism, heart and talent allowing her to possess the title of Greatest Of All Time (GOAT)! Serena cannot maintain playing at such a high level while running her own successful businesses and, more importantly, being a mother and wife if she was not focused on obtaining her goals.

If I could have a conversation with Serena about the masculine words the announcers use when describing her style of play, the body shaming she endured, the racial unfairness shown to her as she rose to super stardom, I would tell her to lift up *her* eyes to the mountains. Where will *her* help come from? *Your* help comes from the Lord, Who made heaven and earth. (italics is my emphasis). Psalms 121:1-2 (NLT) says:

> *I look up to the mountains—does my help come from there? My help comes from the Lord, who made heaven and earth!*

I would let Serena know I believe it is all mental at this stage of her game. When we become mothers, the scope of how we view things is a whole new dynamic. Serena, you are a mother now and when you look across the net at your opponent, you psychologically envision your child. To some degree, your maternal instinct kicks in; but you should be reminded of 1 Peter 5:7 (NIV):

> *Cast all your anxiety on him because he cares for you.*

Adjusted Focus

Kobe is my favorite basketball player. Kobe was relentless and sustained a high level of focus in all his endeavors. I watched him play with such intensity and tenacity, often referred to as his 'mamba mentality.' Kobe had a ferocious spirit on the basketball court and he also expressed this in his award-winning, poignant writings. 1 Timothy 4:16 (NASB) says:

> *Pay close attention to yourself and to your teaching; persevere in these things, for as you do this you will ensure salvation both for yourself and for those who hear you.*

Staying Focused

As Kobe transitioned from the game of basketball, I had to find my next passionate player. Damian 'Dame Dolla' Lillard fits the bill perfectly. He has a quiet demeanor, but his game is monstrous! His journey to the National Basketball Association (NBA) is a story that made me admire him even more. Damian knew he must stay focused as he has his eye on a bigger prize—an NBA championship. Romans 12:2 (NLT) says:

> *Don't copy the behavior and customs of this world, but let God transform you into a new person by changing the way you think. Then you will learn to know God's will for you, which is good and pleasing and perfect.*

Watch and See Focused

I am perplexed as why do football players and track runners look back instead of focusing on what is ahead of them—the goal-line, or the finish line. I scratch my head and wonder why they will not tune into their other senses, such as hearing, to reach their determined destination by looking forward.

Lot's wife disobeyed the Angel's condition, 'do not look back'. She looked back and was transformed into a pillar of salt. She had a longing for what was behind her and instead of focusing on the promise in front of her. (Read Genesis 19:26)

Lamar Jackson is poetry in motion on the football field. He patiently and vehemently allowed his talent to speak to all his naysayers, stating "I am the best." He believed in himself. He embodied and owned the game as he flourished; he lived focused on the gridiron. Lamar has incomparable responsibility and a powerful opportunity to lead on and off the turf. Proverbs 4:25 (NKJV) says:

> *Let your eyes look straight ahead, And your eyelids look right before you.*

Living Focused

Zion Williamson is the WOW of basketball. I made it a priority to watch Zion play at Duke. He lived focused on the court. Zion has a lot to carry at such a young age as he is eminently the future of basketball. This young man reflects such a positive image instilled in him by his mother. Zion's mother saw his potential and nurtured his abilities.

Zion's humbling spirit and physical charisma will take him far in the NBA as his talents will progress prodigiously. Matthew 6:34 (NLT) says:

> *So don't worry about tomorrow, for tomorrow will bring its own worries. Today's trouble is enough for today.*

I have had several Pastors comment in their sermons about a member shouting for their favorite sport(s) and will sit on God in the church pew quiet and reserved. I found myself convicted of such actions. I love my sports, but I love my Lord more! Although I have days where I am fist pumping and yelling 'Come On'; my trust to carry me through is strictly in the hands of the Lord. I lift my hands in reverence of my Father. I will not be silent on Him! Isaiah 26:3 (NIV) says:

> *You will keep in perfect peace those whose minds are steadfast, because they trust in you.*

Moment of Truth	Song
Focus first on God Himself; be practical indeed. And as you tell the world of Christ, you will find He will meet your need! Jill Briscoe - 1580 (NKJV, The Woman's Study Bible)	Alabaster Box by CeCe Winans

PRAYER

Thank You for allowing me to witness greatness in Your children. Thank You for giving me the opportunity to live vicariously through the athletic talents of my favorite athletes. I appreciate You letting me know where my talents lie and getting to know and appreciate sports in my life.

Joy

> James 1:17 (NLT)
>
> Whatever is good and perfect is a gift coming down to us from God our Father, who created all the lights in the heavens. He never changes or casts a shifting shadow.

Joy

My son whom I adore to the utmost and find great joy; was a blessing of my teen hormonal hotness chaos, created to survive in my teen mindset. My son is a smooth dancer. I love to watch him and especially to dance with him.

I first saw my son dance as a young adult when he served as an escort for our local Beautillion. There was a ball dance he attended every year around November. He was also a Beau for his own Beautillion and he showed out working those dance moves! He would make it a point to dance with the older women. They would come back and tell me what a smooth dancer and what a gentleman he was to them. That made me smile and it brought me joy.

My son has a dimpled smile that brings joy to others. My son was athletic. My son and I worked for the same organization. He would walk down to my office just to give me a hug and kiss, and would bebop back to his work area. Lovingkindness; that's joy!

Psalms 92:4 (NLT) says:

You thrill me, Lord, with all you have done for me! I sing for joy because of what you have done.

Joyful

My middle child whom I adore to the utmost and find great joy; was a blessing from a marriage I entered into, trying to run away from the Military Sexual Trauma (MST) I endured at the hand of leadership. When she was born, she came out looking at me with eyes wide open and ready for the world.

My middle child is also the middle grandchild. We have done so much together. When she was invited to a social event, she could have taken a date if she wanted to, but she would rather hang out with her mom instead. I was taken aback when she asked to go to a Historically Black College and University (HBCU) that was 13 hours away from our home. I said, "Girl you can barely go across the street without me, and you want to go to school 13 hours away??"

My middle child, no matter how hard I tried, was not athletic! To help with releasing her drama talent, I signed her up to audition for the local children's play theater. She was indeed my drama queen. And when she had an issue with aggression, I enrolled her in martial arts. We did however finally find her niche during a Show Choir while waving flags in a marching band: she loved to dance and sing.

My middle child has a kind heart. She will give you her last, once. She serves as the nucleus of our immediate family. My middle child was only 8 years old when she began working for my Dad's barbeque business. She had no concept of money; so, my dad saved her wages for her. Because the middle child had great customer service skills, she made incredibly good tips at my dad's business. On occasion, she would offer her balled up tip money to me for the household. Unselfishness; that's joy!

John 15:11 (NIV) says:

I have told you this so that my joy may be in you and that your joy may be complete.

Joyous

My baby whom I adore to the utmost and find great joy; was a blessing of a marriage I thought was oh so real. I sincerely thought my husband loved me. Hear me ladies, be careful what you ask for. I prayed for a 'knight in shining armor'. I later learned a huge lesson — because my former husband's armor was so bright, I could not encounter the real him, ever.

My baby was born a preemie, two months early. She came into this world breathing on her own. She was so tiny; she fit into the palm of my hand. Once I was discharged from labor and delivery, I traveled back to the hospital daily to bond with her; I could not hold her for four weeks.

She finally came home two weeks later. She was sickly. They put her through a stress test that made me want to throw a chair through the window and rescue my child from their medical torture, but I knew it was necessary. My baby had double hernias and had to have surgery. She had a hole in her heart. By the time she was two years old, that ailment had disappeared… poof, gone!

She was an observant child. She would not talk until she was almost 18 months old, but she was a sponge soaking up everything. My baby had many talented gifts. My baby is a real smart cookie! She is athletic. She participated in track, volleyball, basketball and poms. She gave her best in everything she did. She saw how I struggled as a single parent to pay for her sister to attend college/nursing school; she did not want to put me through that with her. She received a full academic/athletic (pole vault) scholarship to attend an HBCU 12 hours away. Determination; that's joy! Psalms 107:22 (NIV) says:

Let them sacrifice thank offerings and tell of His works with songs of joy.

Joy...Joy...Joy

I love my children equally. They are each unique and special in their own way. I cannot treat my oldest like my middle child or my middle child like my baby because they each have distinctive personalities. I had to parent accordingly because of their separate uniqueness.

God made each of us to be unique. The Lord knows about all our quirks. We bring Him so much joy when our journey aligns with His Will for our lives. James 1:2-4 (NLT) says:

> *[2] Dear brothers and sisters, when troubles of any kind come your way, consider it an opportunity for great joy. [3] For you know that when your faith is tested, your endurance has a chance to grow. [4] So let it grow, for when your endurance is fully developed, you will be perfect and complete, needing nothing.*

Rejoice

I can rejoice Christ because You bring me so much joy deep in my soul! 1 Thessalonians 5:16-18 (NIV) says:

> *[16] Rejoice always, [17] pray continually, [18] give thanks in all circumstances; for this is God's will for you in Christ.*

Moment of Truth	Song
Love for the Joy of Loving	Joy by The Georgia Mass Choir

PRAYER

Father, lead me to live in Your righteousness where I will find peace and joy. When my mind is stayed on You, Lord, I find strength to make it one more day. Thank You for supplying me with knowledge and wisdom guiding me to live my best life, thank You for my family, Lord. You know what is and You knew what was needed for their progression in You! Continue to bless them Father and keep them in Your loving care. In Jesus' Name, Amen

Nourishes

Matthew 5:6 (NIV)

Blessed are those who hunger and thirst for righteousness, for they will be filled.

Bear Fruit

God has selected us to be His disciples, and when we embody Him well, we bear good fruit in our lives. We can no longer strut around with our noses held high in the air as we sit in the pew with bible in lap citing our thee and thous; we have to walk His walk and talk His talk! We ought to have the fruit to back it up. John 15:1-5 (NIV) says:

[1] I am the true vine, and my Father is the gardener. [2] He cuts off every branch in me that bears no fruit, while every branch that does bear fruit he prunes so that it will be even more fruitful. [3] You are already clean because of the word I have spoken to you. [4] Remain in me, as I also remain in you. No branch can bear fruit by itself; it must remain in the vine. Neither can you bear fruit unless you remain in me. [5] I am the vine; you are the branches. If you remain in me and I in you, you will bear much fruit; apart from me you can do nothing.

Proverbs 3:8 (NIV) says:

This will bring health to your body and nourishment to your bones.

Increase Godly Knowledge

We must understand it is God who gives us the gift of knowledge. By His Word we gain wisdom and insight into His plan for our lives. To develop a closer relationship with our Father we must study to show ourselves approved daily. **Proverbs 2:6 (NIV)** says:

> *For the Lord gives wisdom; from his mouth come knowledge and understanding.*

Proverbs 18:15 (NIV) says:

> *The heart of the discerning acquires knowledge, for the ears of the wise seek it out.*

Find Strength in Power

We are thankful for the wonder working power of God in our lives. God gives us the strength, ability, and wisdom we need to finish strong in His Name. We are stronger than we ever imagined. In unity there is strength. Isaiah 40:29 (NIV) says:

> *He gives strength to the weary and increases the power of the weak.*

Ephesians 6:10 (NIV) says:

> *Finally, be strong in the Lord and in His mighty power.*

Remain Steadfast

Stand firm in faith, unmovable and hold on to the truth. Stay focused on what He has called you to do. Be still and know God will direct you to where He wants you to be. Proverbs 16:3 (NLT) says:

> *Commit your actions to the Lord, and your plans will succeed.*

Be Patient

We need to keep waiting on God and trusting Him with plain ole faith. When we stop believing we can figure it out on our own and turn it over to Him — God will swoop in, He will say, 'It is done', then, drops the mic!

Do not give up! Do not stop believing! Stay full of confidence 'expecting the expected'. God's power is unlimited, and He is faithful and just to come through for us in His time. Romans 12:12 (NLT) says:

Rejoice in our confident hope. Be patient in trouble, and keep on praying.

Romans 8:25 (NIV) says:

But if we hope for what we do not yet have, we wait for it patiently.

Moment of Truth	Song
Your Inner Self Needs External Nourishment	Fill Me Up by Casey J Fill Me Up by Tasha Cobb

PRAYER

Father, please create in me a humble heart, mind and soul. I rely on You for my strength daily. Thank You for working through me in remarkable ways, in spite of my shortcomings. Father, I will be steadfast as You provide me the ability to nurture the good fruit You provide in my life so I can embody You to those around me. Thank You for guidance and grace to reveal Your love to others daily. In Your Son's Precious Name, Amen

Overwhelmed

Isaiah 54:17 (NLT)

But in that coming day no weapon turned against you will succeed. You will silence every voice raised up to accuse you. These benefits are enjoyed by the servants of the Lord; their vindication will come from me. I, the Lord, have spoken!

Pray Your Way Through It

Overwhelmed with sickness and disease, unhappiness, poverty, loneliness, a broken home, workplace frustration and complexities, unemployment, fear and depression, or shattered relationships. The remedy is to pray to the Father, and when you pray, pray knowing He is working it out for you.

God answers prayer, not in our time, but in His time. Hold strongly to the Word of God. James 5:16 (NKJV) says:

Confess your trespasses to one another, and pray for one another, that you may be healed. The effective, fervent prayer of a righteous man avails much.

During times of trouble, trials of tribulations, Jesus is intervening for your sake. He is petitioning our Heavenly Father and advocating for your individual blessings.

Romans 3:23 (NIV) says:

...for all have sinned and fall short of the glory of God.

But be mindful, each day He shields us from hurt, harm or dangers —seen and unseen. Romans 8:34 (NIV) says:

Who then is the one who condemns? No one. Christ Jesus who died —more than that, who was raised to life—is at the right hand of God and is also interceding for us.

Scope Out the Offender

The enemy knows your Achilles heel. The tempter knows that pointing out your avenging attitude, revealing your ever-evolving emotionally-charged aggression, illuminating your fragile low self-esteem, shining the light on your weight gain due to your insatiable appetite for peach cobbler, or that dark cloud of gloom in the workplace due to lack of trust, or the late-night creep because you are lusting for Mr. Good Guy. Luke 20:43 (NLT) says:

…until I humble your enemies, making them a footstool under your feet.

Romans 16:20 (NLT) says:

The God of peace will soon crush Satan under your feet. May the grace of our Lord Jesus be with you.

Satan knows all of your pet peeves, like when the fast food drive-through clerk messes up your order and you do not check the container before you pull off; you get home and hit the roof because the order is messed up or missing a valued dipping sauce! I am talking to the real foodies out there. 1 Peter 5:8 (NIV) says:

Be alert and of sober mind. Your enemy the devil prowls around like a roaring lion looking for someone to devour.

There are moments when all that is good can turn into a trickle down effect of bad, I come to tell you do not worry ladies, God is able to understand our weaknesses.

Hebrews 4:15 (NIV) says:

For we do not have a high priest who is unable to empathize with our weaknesses, but we have One who has been tempted in every way, just as we are – yet He did not sin.

Reality Check Please

You will worry about this, that and the other. You worry about worries you cannot control. You will allow worry to fester inside which will eventually manifest itself on your outside. Anxiety is a distraction keeping you from focusing on God's plan for you right now.

Do not worry about anything; but pray about everything. God desires for you to talk with Him daily. Whether you hear from Him or not, say Thank You Lord anyhow! When you turn it over to God, you will experience Godly peace; a peace unlike anything we could comprehend. Philippians 4:6-7 (MSG) says:

Don't fret or worry. Instead of worrying, pray. Let petitions and praises shape your worries into prayers, letting God know your concerns. Before you know it, a sense of God's wholeness, everything coming together for good, will come and settle you down. It's wonderful what happens when Christ displaces worry at the center of your life.

The storms of life are inevitable ladies. A fact of life is you have to go through some things; and when you do, you must allow them to filter through to culminate God's promises. His Words are unbreakable, making your hope unshakable. Romans 15:13 (NIV) says:

May the God of hope fill you with all joy and peace as you trust in Him, so that you may overflow with hope by the power of the Holy Spirit.

Leap Into Action

God has the whole world covered and that includes covering you too! He knows everything about you. He will never leave nor forsake you! Nothing can separate you from the love of God! Psalms 139:4 (NLT) says:

You know what I am going to say even before I say it, Lord.

Leave your worries with God. Believe me, He has it all under control. God is powerful all by Himself! He simply wants to love you, and for you to love Him.

Lean on the Father. Ask Him for help. Just have a little talk with Him. He never leaves you nor forsakes you. Deuteronomy 31:6 (NIV) says:

Be strong and courageous. Do not be afraid or terrified because of them, for the Lord your God goes with you; he will never leave you nor forsake you.

If you would just be still and realize you are just a prayer away from your blessing... from your breakthrough! Psalms 46:10 (NKJV) says:

Be still, and know that I am God; I will be exalted among the nations, I will be exalted in the earth!

I am so glad Father, there are no surprises with You. You are the same today and will be the same tomorrow. I find comfort in the fact You are unshakable, and nothing is greater, bigger, or stronger than You. Open my eyes Lord; make it plain for me see that the problems I face today pale in comparison to how big You are.

Colossians 1:16–17 (MSG) says:

We look at this Son and see the God who cannot be seen. We look at this Son and see God's original purpose in everything created. For everything, absolutely everything, above and below, visible and invisible, rank after rank after rank of angels—everything got started in Him and finds its purpose in Him. He was there before any of it came into existence and holds it all together right up to this moment. And when it comes to the church, He organizes and holds it together, like a head does a body.

Moment of Truth	Song
Do not let minor worries overwhelm you! Do not sweat the small stuff!	His Eye is on the Sparrow by Lauryn Hill & Tanya Blount All in His Plan by PJ Morton featuring Le'andria Johnson & Mary Mary

PRAYER

Father, in the Name of Jesus, I thank You for the spirit of courage and revelation that I can restrict and stop the movement of the lows in my life. I do not have to be overwhelmed but I can be of good courage because of You. I am confident my troubles will not triumph over me. In the Name of Jesus, I rebuke sickness and disease, unhappiness, poverty, loneliness, broken homes, workplace frustration and complexities, unemployment, fear and depression, and unhealthy relationships. I will no longer let the strongholds of embarrassment or disappointment bind me. You, Lord, have set me free. I release the chains that keep me bogged down with worry. I lay it all on the alter God. When life is overwhelming, Lord I trust You! In the Name of Jesus, Amen

Ripples

> Proverbs 3:5-6 (KJV)
>
> Trust in the Lord with all thine heart; and lean not unto thine own understanding. In all thy ways acknowledge him, and he shall direct thy paths.

The ripples of your life choices continue for good or will splish splash long after that choice was originally made. The choices you have made in the past and the choices we are yet to make, will immensely coincide with and affect your future generations.

Drop a pebble in water and watch the wonders of its rippling motion. Visualize how the ripples continue on and on and on. The ripple appears to be never ending. Some rippling effects in our lives are not as tranquil and can cause irreparable pain, hurt and damage.

I introduce to you, my ripple effect...

▸ Joined Military service to provide for my son to become financially secure. I was working five jobs before I joined.

▸ Asked Military leadership if I could send for my son. I was told when I reached my duty station, my son would be able to come and live with me.

▸ At the first duty station, I requested permission from military leadership about sending for my son to come and live with me.

▸ Military leadership indicated, for my son to come and live with me, I had to perform some tasks. Pass room inspection, done; attain E-4 Specialist rank, done. The next task military leadership wanted me to do was to perform a sexual act he called 'topping him off'.

▸ I encountered continuous and excessive sexual abuse from Military leadership.

▸ Military leadership revealed I would be left alone (no more sexual 'topping him off') if I was to get married to someone.

Proverbs 3:5-6 (NLT) says:

> *Trust in the Lord with all your heart; do not depend on your own understanding. Seek His will in all you do, and He will show you which path to take.*

▸ Married my 'homeboy' to avoid sexual abuse from Military leadership.

▸ Son came to live with us.

▸ Encountered verbal, physical and mental abuse from former husband.

▸ Endured because I felt it was my fault; I married former husband for all the wrong reasons.

▸ Sent son back home to live with my parents.

▸ Stayed with former husband at my next duty station.

▸ Became pregnant with middle child.

▸ Divorced former husband.

Romans 8:28 (NLT) says:

> *And we know that God causes everything to work together for the good of those who love God and are called according to his purpose for them.*

▸ Second husband divorced me because I was not 'freaky' enough.

▸ Raised children as a single parent.

▸ Kept each child busy so I would be busy, and my focus would always be on them and never on me and my past pain.

▸ Son grew up. Middle child went to college. Baby girl went to college.

▸ My health, mind, body and soul began to fail.

▸ The trauma I suffered surfaced and erupted inside of me. Lord, my God the excruciating pain of it all! This led to my diagnosis of suffering from depression and Post Traumatic Stress Disorder-Military Sexual Trauma (PTSD-MST).

Galatians 5:1 (MSG) says:

> *Christ has set us free to live a free life. So take your stand! Never again let anyone put a harness of slavery on you.*

The Holy Spirit takes up residence in us once we are saved. The Holy Spirit convicts us. The Holy Spirit reminds us to do all and be all God has intended us to be. God has given the Holy Spirit authority over us as we desire to grow into His likeness and Godly attributes. Psalms 147:15 (NIV) says:

> *He sends His command to the earth; His word runs swiftly.*

Moment of Truth	Song
When we…Know whose we are…(in Christ) It leads to…Knowing who we are…(in Christ) Concludes with…Knowing why we are…(Purpose in Christ)	You Know My Name by Tasha Cobbs

PRAYER

Thank You, Father, Son and the Holy Spirit. I love You; Use me to do Your Will. Lord, may the rippling effect You have in and on my life trickle down to those I love and those You intend for me to bless! In Jesus' Name, Amen

Psalms 100:2 (NIV)

Worship the Lord with gladness; come before Him with joyful songs.

*C*lose your eyes. Take a deep breath. Now I want you to visualize the song that makes you wanna sing and move rhythmically at the stoplight or when waiting on a train to pass or when waiting to pick up your child from after school activities. That song that strikes a memory chord and produces a reactive grin and, in turn, it takes you way, way back. Now, hold on to that memory!

When my girls were younger, I would jam to a song in the car and they would sarcastically say to me, "You do know your windows are NOT tinted"—meaning others can see you Mom. Oh, well, it only embarrassed them. My girls would also try and slyly throw in a jib jab while I was singing at church, they would tell me to pick a key and stay with it.

Little did they know, I was not giving their comments any attention because it was my opportunity to praise and worship in my own way. Ephesians 5:19 (NLT) says:

> *...singing Psalms and hymns and spiritual songs among yourselves, and making music to the Lord in your hearts.*

My water aerobics instructor would play a variety of music during our workout sessions. I would especially perk up when a song by The Chainsmokers featuring Halsey called 'Closer' came on the radio. I loved the upbeat, uplifting, and urban sound.

Pharrell's song 'Happy' from the animated movie 'Despicable Me 2', will get a reactionary rhythmic shimmy from me every time — no matter where I am. When this song came on the radio, I would turn it up and encourage my co-workers to stop what they were doing and take a shimmy (dance) break. Most would comply and we would have a good laugh. I would go to their offices without having heard the song and just start to shimmy with a co-worker to encourage them to shake it loose, girl. Let it go! Release it! James 5:13 (NIV) says:

> *Is anyone among you in trouble? Let them pray. Is anyone happy? Let them sing songs of praise.*

It really saddens me when I hear an all-around great beat to a song on the radio, but when I go to download the song, I am soured on the song for its blatant degradation of sexual overtones towards women leaving nothing to the listeners' imagination. The song's lyrics include every profanity known to man on God's green earth, which in my opinion, vehemently takes away from the smooth sound and banging beat. The derogatory lyrics regarding women in some songs is absolutely unacceptable.

I love all types of music. I love songs that are lyrically sound. I love music that has a memorable melody. I love all genres of music! Psalms 96:1 (NKJV) says:

> *Oh, sing to the Lord a new song! Sing to the Lord, all the earth.*

When you are brokenhearted, weary, despondent, or lacking your umph for the day. I implore you to find that one song that brings back those nostalgic memories to put a smile on your beautiful face. Go to a room in your house where you can sway and move to the supersonic sound of this song. Relax and let all inhibitions flow freely from your mind, body and soul.

My girls would climb into a chair and just watch me dance around my living room to all types of music. I recommend doing a mental and physical cleansing with song and dance at least twice a week. Just saying. Psalms 51:17 (NLT) says:

The sacrifice you desire is a broken spirit. You will not reject a broken and repentant heart, O God.

Having a relationship with the Lord will keep you desiring for a deeper dynamic compelling you to long for moments of prolific praise and wondrous worship with gospel songs or your favorite hymn. Those moments on Sunday mornings at church are elevating, but when it is just me and the Lord, girl I am talking about a mighty good time in Him!

Singing songs to honor and give glory to my Lord just has a way of carrying away life's trials and tribulations. I am renewed and refocused with my mind staying on Him!

Psalms 149:1 (NIV) says:

Praise the Lord. Sing to the Lord a new song, His praise in the assembly of His faithful people.

Colossians 3:16 (NLT) says:

Let the message of Christ, in all its richness, fill our lives. Teach and counsel each other with all the wisdom He gives. Sing Psalms and hymns and spiritual songs to God with thankful hearts.

Moment of Truth	Song
Remembering Happiness is Like Enjoying it Twice	Why We Sing by Kirk Franklin

PRAYER

Dear Lord, thank You for allowing me to sing songs that make me happy and the songs that give You the glory, honor and praise. You have instilled in me discernment of what is right and wrong. Lord, I know when I sing a song to You it does not miss the mark. Your Holy Spirit engulfs me and brings upon me Your blessed blissfulness! I sing Dear Lord because I am happy! In Jesus' Name, Amen

Sorrow

Psalms 13:2 (NIV)

How long must I wrestle with my thoughts and day after day have sorrow in my heart? How long will my enemy triumph over me?

Sorrow

My dad called me early one Sunday morning, and he said words I did not expect. He said, '(my daughter) had been shot.' That was all he said. I can only assume he was in shock as I was after he told me over the phone. I arose and got dressed. I was numb. I made my way to the hospital emergency room. Upon arrival, I checked in with the nurse at the front desk. She then led me to my daughter's room.

There was a police officer outside of her hospital room door, holding her clothes in a bag. I did not have any information before I turned the corner to enter her room. I did not know what to expect. I entered the room and my dad, who is a U.S. Marine Corps Veteran, was standing at attention by her side. I don't even think he realized I was there.

I approached my daughter. The nursing staff had cleaned her up and was preparing to transport her to another medical facility that could handle her injuries. I stroke her hair and face. Her eyes were not open and formed a slitting look on her face. She uttered 'mom' and her daughter's name. I was then told she had been shot five times. She was at a private establishment with a group of associates when a person decided to shoot up and around the whole building structure. She had to be transported for emergency surgery at a hospital about 45 minutes away. I was numb. Psalms 13:2 (NLT) says:

How long must I struggle with anguish in my soul, with sorrow in my heart every day? How long will my enemy have the upper hand?

Sorrowful

I walked out of the hospital into the parking lot. I did not know who to call or what to do next. I was numb. I called my brother and told him what had happened. He and his wife lived in the city where the hospital was located, and they met my daughter at the hospital before her surgery. I had to pick up my mom from her home and then we both went to my daughter's home to wake the babysitter and retrieve my granddaughter.

I was numb. I drove my parents and my granddaughter to the hospital where my daughter was having surgery. My granddaughter lightheartedly said, "Grandma, why are we going so slow?" I chuckled to myself because I had no idea I was driving slowly on the interstate. I was numb. Romans 5:3-4 (NLT) says:

We can rejoice, too, when we run into problems and trials, for we know that they help us develop endurance. And endurance develops strength of character, and character strengthens our confident hope of salvation.

Angst

Two weeks following my daughter's shooting, I was on my way to work one morning and I started to let myself feel. I began to sob heavily, while driving to work. During this sobbing while driving, I began to push on the car's gas pedal and accelerated at a high rate of speed. I was crying, speeding and talking to God. I saw the sheriff's car turn around. I knew it was me he was going to stop for speeding. I had pulled over and sought my driver's license and insurance card immediately. I sobbingly told him what had been going on in my life regarding my daughter. I just knew I was going to get a speeding ticket. He came back to the car and told me to just be careful and slow down… and let me go.

You see, all this time God had been carrying me. I was becoming weak and I was letting my flesh take charge in the moment. God had been my strength and my rock during the shooting and healing of my daughter. Because of our relationship, I understood my Father was letting me know He had my back and He was not going to allow me to give up or give in! Do not get me wrong, it is alright to cry but, in this case, I had no reason to reach back and relive the past of my daughter's shooting. I had to move forward and live in the present. My daughter was progressing. She should have died from her injuries, but Glory be to God, she did not.

Children of faith must remember grieving is only for a season. Psalms 30:5 (NIV) says:

For His anger lasts only a moment, but His favor lasts a lifetime; weeping may stay for the night, but rejoicing comes in the morning.

2 Corinthians 12:9 (NLT) says:

Each time He said, "My grace is all you need. My power works best in weakness." So now I am glad to boast about my weaknesses, so that the power of Christ can work through me.

Sorrowful, Yet I Rejoice

Because my Father was with me before, during and after I endured an intolerable situation, it is then I found comfort in Him; He is forgiving, loving and honest.

God put the right people in place to take care of my daughter. For instance, the nurse that was at the Emergency Department when my daughter arrived had worked with my dad at a factory, and he had also worked with my daughter at the hospital. The Lord healed my daughter and now she is living out His plan for her life and relying on His unfailing grace on her life.

We may not comprehend why God allows trials and tribulations in our lives, but we can put our trust in Him. The Lord loves us and has us in His hands. Knowledge, authority, and understanding are His! Philippians 4:6-7 (NKJV) says:

Be anxious for nothing, but in everything by prayer and supplication, with thanksgiving, let your requests be made known to God; and the peace of God, which surpasses all understanding, will guard your hearts and minds through Christ Jesus.

Moment of Truth	Song
Every Joy has its Sorrow	Stand by Donnie McClurkin

PRAYER

Dear Lord, have mercy on me when I struggle to comprehend seasonal hardships. I hold onto Your unchanging hand during my struggles, pains, trials and tribulations. Lord, please provide Your loving comfort and a peace that surpasses all understanding. I believe wholeheartedly Father that Your Will will be done in my life and I will be mindful to be still long enough to hear Your sweet and soft voice leading and guiding me in my moment of need. In Jesus' Name, Amen

Church Hurt

Ephesians 2:8-10 (NLT)

8. God saved you by his grace when you believed. And you can't take credit for this; it is a gift from God. 9. Salvation is not a reward for the good things we have done, so none of us can boast about it. 10. For we are God's masterpiece. He has created us anew in Christ Jesus, so we can do the good things he planned for us long ago.

Church Hurt #1

- ▸ Served in church for 34 years

- ▸ Married both former husbands at this church

- ▸ Second former husband cheats

- ▸ Second former husband told the pastor while in marriage counseling he was not cheating

- ▸ Church family knew second former husband was cheating and never said a mumbling word

- ▸ Pastor saw second former husband with girlfriend while still married to me

- ▸ The pastor had to humble himself for dismissing my concerns during marriage counseling

- ▸ Because of this church hurt, I left my church

▸ I left this church based on lack of feeling valued by the church members

I should have forgiven them instead of just leaving this church; I should not have allowed my church hurt to manifest itself in my heart. Luke 17:4 (NIV) says:

> *Even if they sin against you seven times in a day and seven times come back to you saying 'I repent,' you must forgive them.*

Ephesians 4:32 (NIV) says:

> *Be kind and compassionate to one another, forgiving each other, just as in Christ God forgave you.*

If I had the relationship I should have had with God, I would have asked for His guidance to rise above church hurt. Hebrews 10:24 (NIV) says:

> *And let us consider how we may spur one another on toward love and good deeds...*

When you encounter church hurt, it can feel like friendly fire at first. You are stunned and shocked but once you get over that initial emotion, you are hurt. The member smiles in your face and then gossips about you in the next breath. And this behavior is repeated Sunday after Sunday. Zechariah 13:6 (NLT) says:

And if someone asks, 'Then what about those wounds on your chest?[a]' he will say, 'I was wounded at my friends' house!'

Church Hurt #2

▸ Part-time church secretary for two Pastors

▸ Was a Sunday School teacher for preschoolers

▸ Praise dance leadership and choreographer

▸ There was no church in the church meetings

I often wanted to bring stones to the church meetings so the *holier than thou* members can cast the first stone—they exhibited sinless, perfect and beyond reproach behavior, but yet threw stones of rage by their actions. Sadly, I never did follow through with trying to bring peace and remind others that we all sin and fall short of the glory of God. Sin is sin!

▸ Because you stand for what is right and just, you become an outcast; no problem

▸ Because you did not gossip and share confidential information to those who tried to manipulate it out of you for their own misinformation spreading; no problem

▸ When a member stood toe-to-toe with you bullying you because you did not side with the church clique; no problem

I had to make the Godly decision after several years of growing in Him to stop living looking in the rearview mirror. Philippians 3:12-14 (MSG) says:

I'm not saying that I have this all together, that I have it made. But I am well on my way, reaching out for Christ, who has so wondrously reached out for me. Friends, don't get me wrong: By no means do I count myself an expert in all of this, but I've got my eye on the goal, where God is beckoning us onward—to Jesus. I'm off and running, and I'm not turning back.

I pray that church folk will be mindful of God's Word regarding bashing a man of God. Psalms 105:15 (NIV) says:

Do not touch my anointed ones; do my prophets no harm.

The Word of God relating to you when your sister sins against you. Matthew 18:15-17 (NIV) says:

[15] "If your brother or sister sins, go and point out their fault, just between the two of you. If they listen to you, you have won them over. [16] But if they will not listen, take one or two others along, so that 'every matter may be established by the testimony of two or three witnesses.' [17] If they still refuse to listen, tell it to the church; and

if they refuse to listen even to the church, treat them as you would a pagan or a tax collector.

Romans 12:3 (KJV) says:

For I say, through the grace given unto me, to every man that is among you, not to think of himself more highly than he ought to think; but to think soberly, according as God hath dealt to every man the measure of faith.

I judged as well as I was judged.

Matthew 7:1-2 (MSG) says:

Don't pick on people, jump on their failures, criticize their faults — unless, of course, you want the same treatment. That critical spirit has a way of boomeranging. It's easy to see a smudge on your neighbor's face and be oblivious to the ugly sneer on your own.

In other words, sweep around your own front door.

Romans 14:12 (NIV) says:

So then, each of us will give an account of ourselves to God.

Proverbs 12:18 (MSG) says:

Rash language cuts and maims, but there is healing in the words of the wise.

Hebrews 12:1 (NLT) says:

Therefore, since we are surrounded by such a huge crowd of witnesses to the life of faith, let us strip off every weight that slows us down, especially the sin that so easily trips us up. And let us run with endurance the race God has set before us.

We may at some point and time experience church hurt. I want you to learn it is not about you, but about growing your relationship with God! So ladies…On your mark…Get set…Let's GROW…

⇒*Read Ephesians 4:4-16 (NIV) — unity and maturity in the Body of Christ*

Moment of Truth	Song
HURT PEOPLE HURT PEOPLE	Pressure by Jonathan McReynolds

PRAYER

Lord, thank You for the healing and hope we find in You! Help us to bring our hurts to You. Teach us to always be mindful of the words we say to others. The Holy Spirit is our Helper, Comforter, Encourager, and Counselor. He is a constant companion in a world where even the connected people speak harm with the tongue. May we abide forever in Your love and help. In Jesus' Name, Amen

Desires

Psalms 37:4 (KJV)

Delight thyself also in the Lord, and He shall give thee the desires of thine heart.

Deepest Desire

My deepest desire was to be a good mom. I was a statistic. I was a teen mom. I worked and cared for my son. I loved my son and only wanted the best for him. I was working five jobs. It was time for him to go to school and my finances were not adding up for me.

An Army recruiter approached me with the best pitch to solve all of my problems. I enlisted in the U.S. Army holding on to what the recruiter told me. I believed him when he said once I was at my first duty station I would be able to send for my son. You see, my deepest desire was to be a good mom. I wanted my son to be proud of me. Besides the military sexual assault from Army leadership, there was the physical, mental and verbal abuse from my first former husband.

I desired to be the best soldier I could be. That was curtailed due to the battle I had to fight within at the hands of military leadership with the demoralizing and demonstrative disgusting behavior on friendly soil.

I desired to be a good mom and to be the best soldier I could be. I was involved in a terrible accident while returning to our Army site from field maneuvers. I was trained one day to drive a deuce and a half truck. On the day we rolled out to the field, I was told instead to drive a deuce and a half truck with a flatbed carrying eight large engines.

I did fine convoying to the field site. On the way back to our home site, I began descending a steep hill which was common in this country. I started to work the air brakes to slow down but nothing happened. The truck accelerated, going faster and faster. I had to make a split decision to manipulate a curve coming up. My choices in this quick turnaround of time were to crash into and go over the embankment, and my truck and all the cargo would pummel the town below, or hit a tree head on with quickened impact.

I chose hit the tree and save the town. I do not remember what happened after I hit the tree. But when I was revived, I could not feel my legs. The engines were scattered all over the interstate. The truck and the flatbed were overturned. The driver side of the canvas covering was completely smashed in. But the passenger side was perfectly intact! I had a Spiritual passenger lady covering and protecting me! My Father dispatched a heavenly angel to protect me during this horrific accident.

By any visual means, I should have been splat on the concrete road. But again, glory to God, listen, I was laying at the foot of the overturned trailer on top of camouflage that had been covering the engines on the flatbed. The camouflage was on the ground. The camouflage was beneath me as if I was placed there. You see, my deepest desire was to raise my son and to provide for him. I should be dead and gone ladies, but God! God kept me!

God knows your concerns, desires and personal interests. Jesus knows you inside and out. The Lord knows you intimately, completely and perfectly; the way you would desire to be known. He understands you wholeheartedly!

He invites you to not only be His followers, but His faithful friend! John 15:15 (NIV) says:

I no longer call you servants, because a servant does not know his master's business. Instead, I have called you friends, for everything that I learned from my Father I have made known to you.

Jeremiah 29:10-11 (MSG) says:

This is God's Word on the subject: "As soon as Babylon's seventy years are up and not a day before, I'll show up and take care of you as I promised and bring you back home. I know what I'm doing. I have it all planned out—plans to take care of you, not abandon you, plans to give you the future you hope for.

Desire

You live daily finding, pointing out, and disguising your imperfections. When you hide them, it only delays Jesus' power to work within the low impacts of your life. When you invite Jesus into the crooked places of your life, He mends, He molds and He maneuvers you in ways to guide you along His path, reaching His purpose and positioning you to accomplish His will for your life.

Very few people are content with how things are in their lives. You must learn to be accepting of yourselves and learn whose you are in Christ Jesus.

You are special! God created you to be universally unique and with the awesome ability to have an intricate and intimate relationship with Him. You are the workmanship of His loving hands. Psalms 139:14 (NIV) says:

I praise you because I am fearfully and wonderfully made; your works are wonderful, I know that full well.

Genesis 1:27 (NIV) says:

So God created mankind in His own image, in the image of God He created them; male and female He created them.

2 Corinthians 12:7-10 (MSG) says:

Because of the extravagance of those revelations, and so I wouldn't get a big head, I was given the gift of a handicap to keep me in constant touch with my limitations. Satan's angel did his best to get me down; what he in fact did was push me to my knees. No danger then of walking around high and mighty! At first I didn't think of it as a gift and begged God to remove it. Three times I did that, and then he told me, "My grace is enough; it's all you need. My strength comes into its own in your weakness."

Once I heard that, I was glad to let it happen. I quit focusing on the handicap and began appreciating gift. It was a case of Christ's strength moving in on my weakness. Now I take limitations in stride, and with good cheer, these limitations that cut me down to size—abuse, accidents, opposition, bad breaks. I just let Christ take over! And so the weaker I get, the stronger I become.

Desires

Sometimes you wrestle with the skin you are in. When those feelings of insecurity creep into your psyches, that's when you can go to the Lord asking Him to teach you to accept how He has made you; asking Him to transform you as you represent Him in this world for His glory. Matthew 6:21 (KJV) says:

For where your treasure is, there will your heart be also.

Psalms 40:8 (NIV) says:

I desire to do your will, my God; you law is within my heart.

Romans 7:18 (NIV) says:

For I know that good itself does not dwell in me, that is, in my sinful nature. For I have the desire to do what is good, but I cannot carry it out.

Hebrews 13:18 (NIV) says:

Pray for us, for we are sure that we have a clear conscience, desiring to act honorably in all things.

Desired

I desired a knight in shining armor. I desired a man that would not mind a woman with two children. I was told men do not want women with children; I wore that yoke for over 12 long years. I met what I thought was the object of my desire. He became my second and former husband. He desired another woman. While separated, he vehemently told me there was no one else.

One day I decided to go to his girlfriend's house. I was numb. I knocked on her door; her son opened it. I felt as if I was in a scene from a Spike Lee movie where you appear to be moving but you are not. I ascended the stairs where I could hear his voice. I rounded the staircase and I heard him say to his girlfriend, 'you are mine and I do not give a explicit--explicit what others say about it.' That's all I needed to hear.

You see, they did not know I was there. He ran after me as I was leaving the house and she chased after him yelling, 'tell her, tell her'. I desired a knight in shining armor not knowing the armor would shine so bright I lost sight of the real person he turned out to be. The Lord protected me that day! All kinds of wrong shoulda, coulda, woulda happened that day, but God! Mark 12:30 (NLT) says:

And you must love the Lord your God with all your heart, all your soul, all your mind, and all your strength.

Psalm 37:4 (KJV) says:

Delight thyself also in the Lord: and he shall give thee the desires of thine heart.

Invite the Lord on your transforming journey. God sees your heart. He is more interested in you than in your performance. God places the right desires in your hearts and then He gives you those desires, if they are according to His Will for your life. God delights in doing both small and large things for you. Receive God's love and mercy and enjoy your journey!

You usually have desires of natural things like success, finances, nice homes and good relationships, but we should also desire spiritual things. We should desire to know God in a deeper and more intimate way, to always display the fruit of the spirit—Love—and to live our lives in a way that pleases Him.

Un-Desirable

Wrong desires will torment you and make you impatient about receiving them, but sanctified desires come with a willingness to wait on God's ways and timing. When you ask Him to take away fleshly desires and replace them with right ones, God gives you desires that agree with His word and align with His righteousness, giving you peace and joy in your life. Genesis 4:7 (NLT) says:

You will be accepted if you do what is right. But if you refuse to do what is right, then watch out! Sin is crouching at the door, eager to control you. But you must subdue it and be its master.

1 John 2:17 (NIV) says:

The world and its desires pass away, but whoever does the will of God lives forever.

Proverbs 22:1 (NIV) says:

A good name is more desirable than great riches; to be esteemed is better than silver or gold.

Psalms 27:4 (NKJV) says:

One thing I have desired of the Lord, That I will seek: That I may dwell in the house of the Lord All the days of my life, To behold the beauty of the Lord, And to inquire in His temple.

Psalms 73:24 (NLT) says:

You guide me with your counsel, leading me to a glorious destiny.

Moment of Truth	Song
Desire nothing that would bring disgrace. We can be confident that His desire to reveal will always be greater than our desire to know – Carrie Anna Pearce	All in His Plan by PJ Morton (featuring Le'Andria Johnson & Mary Mary) Man of Your Word by Maverick City Music (featuring Chandler Moore & KJ Scriven)

PRAYER

Lord, thank You for the healing and hope we find in You! Help us to bring our hurts to You. Teach us to always be mindful of the words we say to others. The Holy Spirit is our Helper, Comforter, Encourager, and Counselor. He is a constant companion in a world where even the connected people speak harm with the tongue. May we abide forever in Your love and help. In Jesus' Name, Amen

D.U.N.K.

(DIVINE UNDERSTANDING NURTURING KINDNESS)

---

2 Timothy 1:7 (NKJV)

For God has not given us a spirit of fear, but of power and of love and of a sound mind.

Most sports enthusiasts love a demonstrative dunk! The fans will cheer ooohhh and ahhhh when they see an awesome alley-oop, a thunderous throw-down tomahawk, a winding windmill, or a baseline dunk where the player sails, and soars and then SLAM DUNK! The crowd goes wild!

To see the athleticism, skill and the intricacy of the prolific, profound, professional, pounding process of the properly planned slam dunk! The dynamic duo that has the connection and communication internally and externally will be successful in having the home and visiting fans on their feet cheering and fist pumping!

When we put God before anything, loving His Son, and allowing the Holy Spirit to work in our daily lives, then we are on the way to slamming and dunking for our Father! Yaasss!

2 Timothy 2:15 (NLT) says:

> *Work hard so you can present yourself to God and receive His approval. Be a good worker, one who does not need to be ashamed and who correctly explains the word of truth.*

He is Directional

In times of sorrow and weariness, seek direction from God, whom you serve—you very much need God's guidance in life. When you depend on yourself to lead you out of a tempting and sinful situation, then you are sorely missing the mark. Our trust should remain solely in Jesus. There is no reason to fear. In dark times turn to Christ, He will never leave you nor forsake you! Trust God's desire to provide guidance for you during your dark days. God loves you dearly, and you can find peace in His loving arms—even when you are faced with temptation, He will direct you! The Lord can meet you at your full court press and do a crossover, fake to the left and lift to the basket, score two points! Psalms 61:2 (NIV) says:

> *From the ends of the earth I call to You, I call as my heart grows faint; lead me to the rock that is higher than I.*

Proverbs 3:5-6 (NLT) says:

> *[5] Trust in the Lord with all your heart; do not depend on your own understanding.*
>
> *[6] Seek His will in all you do, and He will show you which path to take.*

The Scriptures are a daily guide to help keep your body, mind and soul in line with understanding God and His will for your life. You must study to show yourself approved by utilizing the Bible as the amazing tool it is; and when you adhere to the Word of God, you will keep moving forward. Godly discipline comes from love. Through love we are taught to do the right thing. The Lord teaches us to run from sin and to leap toward holiness and Spiritual obedience.

With hard work and dedicated discipline, you can motivate your bodies to run down the court ahead of the opposing team, catch and score before they even realized what has happened! Ephesians 5:1-2 (NKJV) says:

Therefore be imitators of God as dear children. And walk in love, as Christ also has loved us and given Himself for us, an offering and a sacrifice to God for a sweet-smelling aroma.

Proverbs 10:17 (NIV) says:

Whoever heeds discipline shows the way to life, but whoever ignores correction leads others astray.

He is Determined

God's perspective is that you should live for His glory and purpose, not your own. Your devotion should be offered to Him. His desire for your lives and for others is to praise Him! Boasting God's glory as your own life's point-of-view opens up a world of endless possibilities. Only the Lord knows what you will learn about Him and what He desires for you to prosper in this earth. God will teach you what is good for you and He will lead you down the path you should pursue. God wants a true worshipper — one who will worship Him in Spirit and in truth! 1 Corinthians 15:58 (NIV) says:

Therefore, my dear brothers and sisters, stand firm. Let nothing move you. Always give yourselves fully to the work of the Lord, because you know that you labor in the Lord is not in vain.

John 4:23-24 (NIV) says:

Yet a time is coming and has now come when the true worshipers will worship the Father in the Spirit and in truth, for they are the kind of worshipers the Father seeks. 24 God is spirit, and his worshipers must worship in the Spirit and in truth.

Romans 8:37-39 (NKJV) says:

[37] Yet in all these things we are more than conquerors through Him who loved us. [38] For I am persuaded that neither death nor life, nor angels or principalities nor powers, nor things present nor things to come, [39] nor height nor depth, nor any other created thing, shall be able to separate us from the love of God which is in Christ Jesus our Lord.

He is Divine

Your most trying days can drive you to the edge of despair, disappointment and disgust with how stuff is going on in your life. Sometimes your faith journey will develop bumps in the road, but if you maintain faith the size of a mustard seed, you can move mountains and you can intercede on the behalf of others! Because of what He does for you, He will do for others too! You must share His divine story which will be your testimony. Do not face life alone. Let's unite and worship on one accord. 2 Timothy 3:16 (NLT) says:

All Scripture is inspired by God and is useful to teach us what is true and to make us realize what is wrong in our lives. It corrects us when we are wrong and teaches us to do what is right.

Romans 1:20 (NIV) says:

For since the creation of the world God's invisible qualities—His eternal power and divine nature—have been clearly seen, being understood from what has been made, so that people are without excuse.

2 Peter 1:3-4 (NIV) says:

His divine power has given us everything we need for a godly life through our knowledge of Him who called us by His own glory and goodness. Through these He has given us His very great and precious promises, so that through them you may participate in the divine nature, having escaped the corruption in the world caused by evil desires.

Isaiah 55:1-3 (NIV) says:

[1] Come, all you who are thirsty, come to the waters; and you who have no money, come, buy and eat! Come, buy wine and milk without money and without cost. [2] Why spend money on what is not bread, and your labor on what does not satisfy? Listen, listen to me, and eat what is good, and you will delight in the richest of fare. [3] Give ear and come to me; listen, that you may live. I will make an everlasting covenant with you, my faithful love promised to David.

Moment of Truth	Song
To Err is Human, to forgive divine. - Alexander Pope	My Worship is For Real by Bishop Larry D. Trotter & The Holy Spirit Combined Choirs

PRAYER

Loving Father, thank You for being my rock in a weary land. I trust You Lord and I bask in the peacefulness and lovingkindness and rest in You. I desire You to lead me to understanding Your Will for me, while allowing Your Spirit to guide me through the tough moments in life. God, I want my life to be all about You and not about me. Teach me to decrease so that You will be increased in all areas of my life. Teach me to shift for the good of Your Kingdom. Place in me a Divine Understanding Nurturing Kindness towards others. Let me Slam Dunk Your Word on the sisters seeking to know You, so that they do not see me but only see You Lord. In Jesus' Name, Amen

G.O.A.T.

(GREATEST OF ALL TIME)

Jeremiah 10:6 (NIV)

No one is like you, Lord; you are great, and your name is mighty in power.

Connected Commitment

I am a diehard sports fan. I love to watch Serena Williams play tennis. Serena has an intense desire to continue and elevate her dedication and commitment to her profession, she has undoubtedly earned being called the G.O.A.T. athletically. Her accolades are top notch on and off the court.

I appreciate Serena's multi-talents outside of the tennis world. She was criticized for having so many interests beyond tennis. Serena let her actions speak for her. She was not distracted by her other professional endeavors. Her past only made her stronger; fiercer. Serena endured pain physically (tennis injuries), emotionally (racial injustice) and motherly (with the birth of her daughter). Her determination to be at the very top of her game makes her quest not to quit even more awesome!

It can be a challenge to believe God for the great things He has in store for your life. All you need to do is move forward one step at a time. Luke 9:62 (NLT) says:

But Jesus told him, "Anyone who puts a hand to the plow and then looks back is not fit for the Kingdom of God."

Fervent Faith

Simone Biles is a rising G.O.A.T. She embodies a tumbling tenacity that elevates her to the top of the gymnastic world. She is establishing a powerful legacy. Simone has faith in her talents. She has the perseverance to press on in spite of societal struggles. Simone epitomizes a work ethic while maintaining a positive disposition.

You must rely on God in every aspect of your life. You only need faith the size of a mustard seed. Matthew 17:20 (NLT) says:

You don't have enough faith,' Jesus told them. 'I tell you the truth, if you had faith even as small as a mustard seed, you could say to this mountain, 'Move from here to there,' and it would move. Nothing would be impossible.

📖 Faith is the woman with the issue of blood pressing through the crowd to touch the hem of Jesus' garment! (Read Luke 8:43-48)

📖 Ruth took a leap of faith and followed her mother-in-law Naomi! (Read Ruth 1)

📖 Faithfully the widow trusted Elisha and collected the jars from her neighbors and filled them with oil as instructed. (Read 2 Kings 4:1-7)

📖 Faith is working in the dark! Hebrews 11:1 (NIV) says:

Now faith is confidence in what we hope for and assurance about what we do not see.

Jubilant Joy

Rejoice in knowing God will never leave you nor forsake you. Deuteronomy 31:6 (NLT) says:

So be strong and courageous! Do not be afraid and do not panic before them. For the Lord your God will personally go ahead of you. He will neither fail you nor abandon you.

The real joy is seeing a loved one or a family member come to Jesus just as they are. Count it all joy Christ will leave the 99 sheep to find the one lost sheep; and He will celebrate finding you! The body of Christ delights over the one because that one had no hope. Luke 15:7 (NLT) says:

In the same way, there is more joy in heaven over one lost sinner who repents and returns to God than over ninety-nine others who are righteous and haven't strayed away!

Experience the fullness of joy when you remain steadfast in Christ's Word and connecting to the true vine therefore bearing fruit that lasts. (Read John 15:1-17).

True Testimony

A transparent testimony is the revelation you need to move someone to Christ. When you share your personal testimony, you create a bond with the non-believer and that testimony will catch their attention and will pique their curiosity.

My testimony is not your testimony. You are unique in the path you have taken to connect as a child of God. A true testimony is hard to negate because of your personal experience with God. Your true testimony is formulation of your thorough and compelling foundation for what the Lord has already done and will do for you! The believer speaks on the gospel in a powerful way, by responding with strong and specific explanations on what the Lord has done along your journey with their hope centered on Christ Jesus.

1 Peter 1:8-9 (NIV) says:

> *Though you have not seen him, you love him; and even though you do not see him now, you believe in him and are filled with an inexpressible and glorious joy. for you are receiving the end result of your faith, the salvation of your souls.*

The testimony of the church is a testimony to the power of Jesus Christ!

Take care of the possible and trust God with the impossible. God does the impossible because nothing is impossible for Him (Read Luke 1:37).

God has been asking you to do something and you have been resisting. Stop running from your desired purpose on God's green earth! Put your hand to the plow and do not glance back over your shoulder! God will empower you and guide you; He will be with you every step of the way. All Heaven will rejoice when someone surrenders to Jesus. We must seek to do the impossible with God! 1 Thessalonians 5:16-18 (NLT) says:

> *[16] Always be joyful. [17] Never stop praying. [18] Be thankful in all circumstances, for this is God's will for you who belong to Christ Jesus.*

John 16:24 (NKJV) says:

> *Until now you have asked nothing in My name. Ask, and you will receive, that your joy may be full.*

Moment of Truth	Song
Jesus, I am resting, resting in the joy of what thou art; I am finding out the greatness of thy longing heart. – Jean Sophie Pigott, 1876-1903	The Center of My Joy by Richard Smallwood

PRAYER

Father, thank You for teaching me how to live in Your righteousness, peace and joy that are mine in Christ Jesus. Thank You for providing me with the strength I need to live faithfully and joyfully in You. In Jesus' Name, Amen

Grace

Luke 1:78-79 (NIV)

...because of the tender mercy of our God, by which the rising sun will come to us from heaven to shine on those living in darkness and in the shadow of death, to guide our feet into the path of peace.

Grace in Righteousness

Grace rules through righteousness to give eternal life to those that love the Lord. When you submit to Jesus, He provides you with the reward of His righteousness. You are made right with God by faith.

When you have a relationship with Jesus, you can abide in His righteousness. We all fall short of His glory, but God already knows this about His children. I urge you to pray with boldness knowing God hears and answers your prayers. Not because of anything you have done; but because of everything He has done.

In Him and through Him, you are a joint heir to the throne of God. Romans 14:17 (NIV) says:

...but righteousness, peace and joy in the Holy Spirit.

Romans 4:4-5 (NIV) says:

Now to the one who works, wages are not credited as a gift but as an obligation. However, to the one who does not work but trusts God who justifies the ungodly, their faith is credited as righteousness.

Galatians 2:21 (NLT) says:

I do not treat the grace of God as meaningless. For if keeping the law could make us right with God, then there was no need for Christ to die.

1 Peter 2:24 (KJV) says:

Who His own self bare our sins in His own body on the tree, that we, being dead to sins, should live unto righteousness: by whose stripes ye were healed.

Grace in Peace

Paul began most of his letters to the church with, "Grace and peace to you from God our Father and the Lord and Savior Jesus Christ." God's grace is what provides you peace!

Because of His grace, God forgives your sins, which guides you to peace with Him and releases you from guilt.

His grace is sufficient to do all that needs to be done and it is enough to meet all your needs. Trust and believe, He is always working, and He is always right on time.

Jesus desires for you to have His peace in every part of your life. John 14:1 (NLT) says:

Don't let your hearts be troubled. Trust in God, and trust also in me.

Do not allow frustration, sadness, worry, anxiety, fear or doubt, interfere with the peace God desires for your life. Hour by hour, minute by minute, second by second, I want to inspire you to put your trust in God daily.

As you go through the process of releasing your cares on Him, you will find a peace that surpasses all understanding. 2 Corinthians 9:8 (NKJV) says:

> *And God is able to make all grace abound toward you, that you, always having all sufficiency in all things, may have an abundance for every good work.*

Grace in Power

Who gives you a jarring bolt of energy? What plug source does your currant of energy run through?

God wants you to fully plug in to His amazing power that flows from His grace. Unfortunately, negative thoughts cause your mindset to weaken God's power in you. You need God's wonder working power to conquer all your trials, tribulations and obstacles you have endured in your life.

Grace is stronger than your sin, your rebellion and your strongholds.

There is no power shortage in heaven. God's grace is sufficient to meet every need if you allow yourself to be open to His will.

God has all the power you need to do anything you need to do. He loves you and wants to give you His power to live your everyday life with joy. Lean on Him with absolute trust in His wisdom and goodness and live with God-given confidence. Romans 6:14 (NLT) says:

> *Sin is no longer your master, for you no longer live under the requirements of the law. Instead, you live under the freedom of God's grace.*

Grace in Faith

Grace is based on faith. Grace justifies you by faith. Grace centers you in Christ. Grace certifies your freedom. Grace lives in you.

You have been saved by grace, through faith. Unfortunately, too many Christians live their lives according to Galatians 3:3 (NIV):

Are you so foolish? After beginning by means of the Spirit, are you now trying to finish by means of the flesh?

Faith in God creates rest for your soul, allowing you to live simply and freely, the way He wants you to be. Faith does not just happen in your relationship with God, but develops as you get to know Him personally. Take steps of faith and trust His faithfulness. Thank Him in for the perfect and good measure of faith He has given you. It is trust released through the power of prayer and thankfulness. I encourage you to ask God to help you build a deeper trust in Him. Ephesians 2:8-10 (NIV) says:

[8] For it is by grace you have been saved, through faith — and this is not from yourselves, it is the gift of God — [9] not by works, so that no one can boast. [10] For we are God's handiwork, created in Christ Jesus to do good works, which God prepared in advance for us to do.

Grace in Love

The Lord's grace includes unmerited favor, unexpected acceptance, and unconditional love.

Jesus is the giver of grace. God is a giving God. He gives out of His love and He loves to give — grace is one of His greatest joys.

God's Word teaches you to love everyone, including yourself. When you accept God's love and learn to love yourself by seeing yourself through God's eyes, then you will be able to love others the way God loves them.

I know it's easier said than done when you have to love those who treat you badly. God's love is given to us freely. Grace, you cannot earn it and you do not deserve it, yet He willingly and continually yearns to express His love. All you need to do is open your heart, trust in His Word, and accept it with thankfulness. Believe wholeheartedly that God loves you with an eternal love and wants you to share His love with others. 2 Peter 3:18 (NIV) says:

But grow in the grace and knowledge of our Lord and Savior Jesus Christ. To him be glory both now and forever! Amen.

Moment of Truth	Song
We never cry out to God and receive a returned check stamped 'Insufficient Grace' – Sandy Smith, 1724	Forever/Beautiful Grace by Kirk Franklin

PRAYER

Father, Your grace is amazing! Thank You, Lord, that I have the chance to live with Your wisdom and Your Word applied to my life, inside and out. In Your wisdom, You have both saved me and called me to live by grace according to Your purpose. In Jesus' Name, Amen

Midst

> ### John 14:27 (NIV)
>
> Peace I leave with you; My peace I give you. I do not give to you as the world gives. Do not let your hearts be troubled and do not be afraid.

Jesus is the Prince of Peace!

Jesus is peace in the midst of all storms! Turn to Him when faced with life's topsy-turvy situation…! Psalms 28:7 (NIV) says:

The Lord is my strength and my shield; my heart trusts in him, and he helps me. My heart leaps for joy, and with my song I praise him.

Jesus is Shelter in the Midst of the Storm!

Isaiah 32:2 (NIV) says:

Each one will be like a shelter from the wind and a refuge from the storm, like streams of water in the desert and the shadow of a great rock in a thirsty land.

You can turn to Jesus for peace that surpasses all understanding!
You must strive to manifest complete confidence in God's power to
meet your needs—good or bad/big or small. Philippians 4:7 (NLT)
says:

*Then you will experience God's peace, which exceeds anything we
can understand. His peace will guard your hearts and minds as you
live in Christ Jesus.*

Jesus is Lasting Peace!

Exodus 14:14 (NLT) says:

The Lord himself will fight for you. Just stay calm.

God is bigger than any problem you will ever face! When you
submit to His Will and dwell on Him during your plights in life,
you will realize Jesus is the answer because He is the author and
finisher of your faith and you can cast all your cares on Him!

Hebrews 12:2 (KJV) says:

*Looking unto Jesus the author and finisher of our faith; who for the
joy that was set before him endured the cross, despising the shame,
and is set down at the right hand of the throne of God.*

Psalms 55:22 (NLT) says:

*Give your burdens to the Lord, and he will take care of you. He will
not permit the godly to slip and fall.*

1 Peter 5:7 (NLT) says:

Give all your worries and cares to God, for He cares about you.

I know true heartedly, worry will well itself up in even the
strongest of women! I know that discomfort, pain and challenging
circumstances will evolve because of the many hats you wear. But
while you are enduring a let-down, or a detrimental
disappointment, or a deepened distress, I implore you, not to stay

there! Pray profoundly about your concerns to restore confidence; turn it all over to Him. Psalms 30:5 (NKJV) says:

For His anger is but for a moment, His favor is for life; Weeping may endure for a night, But joy comes in the morning.

He will wipe out worry and alter it to Worship!

Joshua 1:9 (NIV) says:

Have I not commanded you? Be strong and courageous. Do not be afraid; do not be discouraged, for the Lord your God will be with you wherever you go.

He will shift your battles into blessings!

2 Chronicles 20:15 (NLT) says:

...This is what the Lord says: Do not be afraid! Don't be discouraged by this mighty army; for the battle is not yours, but God's.

Do not set your mind on the plans, desires or worries of tomorrow!

Matthew 6:34 (MSG) says:

Give your entire attention to what God is doing right now, and don't get worked up about what may or may not happen tomorrow. God will help you deal with whatever hard things come up when the time comes.

God gives you perspective daily!

Matthew 11:28 (NIV) says:

Come to me, all you who are weary and burdened, and I will give you rest.

Psalms 119:105 (KJV) says:

Thy word is a lamp unto my feet, and a light unto my path.

Romans 12:21 (NLT) says:

Don't let evil conquer you, but conquer evil by doing good.

God takes away your worries, anxieties, depression and sadness, and shifts them to joy, peace, hope and love. Reading God's Word and Worshiping God in Spirit and in Truth allows you to draw nearer to Him.

In the midst of adversity; In the midst of storms; In the midst of suffering, troubles, trials, struggles, confusion, criticism, weeping, depression or persecution... Praise Him anyhow!! (Read Psalms 34:1-14)

Moment of Truth	Song
In the Meantime...	In the Midst Of It All by Yolanda Adams In the Middle by Isaac Carree

PRAYER

Father, Thank You for loving me and carrying me in the midst of my storms. I appreciate Your grace for peace during the storms of my life. I reject the spirit of confusion, sorrows and fear. Shower me with your peace in the midst of my trials and tribulations. Have mercy on me and forgive me for all of my complaining. Thank You for your peace that transcends all understanding. In Jesus' Name, Amen

DAY 27

> ### 2 Corinthians 13:14 (MSG)
>
> The amazing grace of the Master, Jesus Christ, the extravagant love of God, the intimate friendship of the Holy Spirit, be with all of you.

It is a slam dunk ladies!! All basketball fans love a good slam dunk! Jesus is a slam dunk when your mind is stayed on Him! Isaiah 26:3 (NIV) says:

You will keep in perfect peace those whose minds are steadfast, because they trust in you.

No need to ponder over who is the greatest; because the Lord our God is the **G.O.A.T.** (Greatest Of All Time)! Psalms 145:3 (MSG) says:

God is magnificent; He can never be praised enough. There are no boundaries to His greatness.

We are never out of God's reach; when the situation warrants it, He will provide a **ram** in the bush!

Whenever you have exhausted all your resources or you find yourself in a difficult situation, please believe, God will send a **ram** in the bush. (Read Genesis 22:12-13)

When you reach a point where you are fed up of being sick and tired of being sick and tired and you have finally reached the end of your internal battle, try God!

When you have determined there is no way to accomplish stuff on our own, that is when you discover you cannot do anything without taking it to the Father first!

Proverbs 3:5-6 (NIV) says:

> *Trust in the Lord with all your heart and lean not on your own understanding; in all your ways submit to him, and he will make your paths straight.*

We have **cried tears** from **church hurt** and suffered from **scars** of a bad relationship, **scars** from losing a job, **scars** of unruly children or **scars** from a fouled-up friendship. In the **midst**, it may not seem like you will heal; but be encouraged, you are His and He is yours and He has you covered by the Blood of the Lamb—His Son, Jesus Christ! Jeremiah 30:16-17 (NIV) says:

> *But all who devoured you will be devoured; all your enemies will go into exile. Those who plunder you will be plundered; all who make spoil of you I will despoil. But I will restore you to health and heal your wounds,' declares the Lord, because you are called an outcast, Zion for whom no one cares.*

James 5:11 (NIV) says:

> *As you know, we count as blessed those who have persevered. You have heard of Job's perseverance and have seen what the Lord finally brought about. The Lord is full of compassion and mercy.*

In the **midst** of your trials, say **thank You** Lord!

In the **midst** of your hurt, say **thank You** Lord!

In the **midst** of adversity, say **thank You** Lord!

In the **midst** of sickness, say **thank You** Lord!

Proverbs 4:20-22 (NIV) says:

[20] My son, pay attention to what I say; turn your ear to my words. [21] Do not let them out of your sight, keep them within your heart; [22] for they are life to those who find them and health to one's whole body.

I will endure life's situations Lord because You are always there for me and You said Your **grace** is sufficient!

2 Corinthians 12:9 (NASB) says:

And He has said to me, "My grace is sufficient for you, for power is perfected in weakness." Most gladly, therefore, I will rather boast [a]about my weaknesses, so that the power of Christ may dwell in me.

Your **desire** is to please God! 1 John 2:17 (NIV) says:

The world and its desires pass away, but whoever does the will of God lives forever.

God loves you so much He sacrificed His one and only Son! Godly ideals illuminate a defeated darkness! God has ultimate understanding on perplexing points of concern! Psalms 143:10 (KJV) says:

Teach me to do thy will; for thou art my God: thy spirit is good; lead me into the land of uprightness.

Jesus became the propitiation for our sins! Jesus is the reason for every season of your life! Jesus is the light of the world!

John 8:12 (NIV) says:

When Jesus spoke again to the people, he said, "I am the light of the world. Whoever follows me will never walk in darkness, but will have the light of life."

The Holy Spirit covers us daily! The Holy Spirit convicts and counsels! The Holy Spirit vexes when vulnerable! Isaiah 61:1 (NKJV) says:

The Spirit of the Lord God is upon Me, Because the Lord has anointed Me To preach good tidings to the poor; He has sent Me to heal the brokenhearted, To proclaim liberty to the captives, And the opening of the prison to those who are bound.

Moment of Truth	Song
Two birds in the bush is still two birds in the bush	No Bondage by Jubilee

PRAYER

Dear Lord, I thank You for this day! A day like no other! You have kept me safe and surrounded me with Your lovingkindness. I love You Lord! Thank You for making a way out of no way! In Your wealth of wisdom You saw fit to place a ram in the bush so that no hurt, harm or danger overcame me. This is the day You have made Lord God! I am going to rejoice and be glad in it! In Jesus' Name, Amen

Scars

> Ecclesiastes 3:1-10 (NIV)
>
> There is a time for everything, and a season for every activity under the heavens...

I allowed myself to be devalued, resulting in a trickle-down effect of moments: I married my homeboy from Illinois. I went from the frying pan into the depths of the fire—I left the abuse of military leadership to endure another trauma to my mind, body and soul.

My former husband's abuse consisted of cheating with a person he amusingly referred to as Dirty D.

We lived off-post overseas in a faraway country. We had to drive quite far to reach the barracks during a call-in where we had to report within a certain amount of time. Once we were done with reporting, my former husband would take off in the car and leave me behind with no way to get home and no money to take a cab. I had to walk over the river and through the woods to get to my home, and I am not being dramatic.

Although my former husband did not value me, God valued me enough to light my path and kept me safe from harm on those long walks home.

Isaiah 54:17 (NLT) says:

But in the coming day no weapon turned against you will succeed. You will silence every voice raised up to accuse you. These benefits are enjoyed by the servants of the Lord; their vindication will come from me. I, the Lord, have spoken!

I allowed my former husband to silence me when we were together. I was to be seen and not heard. If for some crazy reason I drummed up the courage to articulate a comment in a conversation, the consequences would escalate when we returned to the car. He would slam my face into the passenger side window. The passersby lowered themselves to window level to see what was going on, then proceeded about their business as if they saw nothing. By the grace of God, the window never shattered. 1 Timothy 4:8 (NIV) says:

For physical training is of some value, but godliness has value for all things, holding promise for both the present life and the life to come.

My former husband kicked in the door of our third-floor apartment. To avoid him, I would grab my son and we would run to the back of the apartment and hunch down in a corner on the balcony. I had no clue how he did not find us. But now I know the Lord was protecting us from the snare of the enemies' attack. The Lord shielded us from the harm that could have befell my son and me.

God's hiding places for me included:

☞ Upstairs in the landlord's apartment — she gave me safe shelter until my former husband left;

☞ Hiding in a dryer — I was much smaller than I am now, for sure.

I think back and have nightmares about what if the dryer door had been shut while I was in there. I did not think to leave my fingers out to prevent it from closing. I just wanted to prevent encountering him not knowing what mood he was in. My Father kept me safe and sent His angels to hide me;

☞ Behind a wood pile in the yard—I could hear his car flying down the graveled driveway and I would run and hide behind the wood pile. Not one time did he find me. I was truly hidden in plain sight. But God!

The abuse of course was getting worse. He tried to drown me in the bathtub. While mad and intoxicated, he would place a chokehold on me resulting in unconsciousness. Psalms 27:5 (NIV) says:

> *For in the day of trouble He will keep me safe in his dwelling; He will hide me in the shelter of His sacred tent and set me high upon a rock.*

My former husband made a makeshift gun from stolen parts from the armory. He pulled the makeshift gun on me in our apartment and pointed it to my head and threatened me. I was so scared I lost my bodily function. That day, Sugar Honey Iced Tea saved me. He called me names and laughed at me on his way out the door as I cried and crawled to the bathroom.

He pulled the makeshift gun on a guy on Post at the NCO club one night. This action led to his arrest, busted down from E-4 grade to E-1 ranking grade, and discharged from the military service. Proverbs 10:20 (MSG) says:

> *The speech of a good person is worth waiting for; the blabber of the wicked is worthless.*

I valued my son enough to send him back home to my parents. I had to make sure my son was safe and that he did not have to see his mommy in distress anymore.

One evening, I was sitting on my bed eating a steak dinner with a steak knife. He entered the room and began to hit me in the face. I had an out-of-body experience. I was looking down at myself getting punched in the face and over my body. Once I reconnected with myself, my mindset was of a woman fed up! I took the steak knife and I started to slash him back and forth—slicing and slashing continuously. He went screaming into the bathroom and locked the door.

Once I calmed down, I felt remorse. I had never hurt anyone with a weapon in my life. So I did not feel good about myself. I should have felt vindicated, triumphant and relieved. But I did not. I coaxed him out of the bathroom and took care of his superficial wounds.

I believe this was the beginning of me feeling free and realizing I had value. I did not deserve this abuse anymore. Matthew 6:26 (NIV) says:

> *Look at the birds of the air; they do not sow or reap or store away in barns, and yet your heavenly Father feeds them. Are you not much more valuable than they?*

Moment of Truth	Song
…A scar is what happens when the Word is made flesh. - Leonard Cohen	Something Has to Break by Kierra Sheard/Tasha Cobb Leonard
Scars are not signs of weakness, they are signs of survival and endurance. - Rodney A. Winters	No Weapon by Fred Hammond & Radical For Christ

PRAYER
Lord, You have brought me a mighty long way! You covered me and protected me when I did not know You as well as I should have. When I look back over my life and I think things over dear heavenly Father I can truly say that I am blessed, Your story is my testimony! Thank You for spreading Your wings and keeping me safe from pending hurt, harm or danger. Thank You for dispatching Your angels to protect me from an abusive relationship. You are my Healer, my Savior and all to You I owe, my Lord! In Jesus' Name, Amen

Tears Crying

Psalms 30:5 (NIV)

For his anger lasts only a moment, but his favor lasts a lifetime;
weeping may stay for the night, but rejoicing comes in the morning.

ears are treasured! Rachel bawled; the woman with the alabaster ointment shed tears; Mary Magdalene wailed; Hannah sobbed; Hagar cried; Mary Mother of Jesus moaned a mournful cry; and JESUS WEPT. (Read John 11:35)

Tears are a language God recognizes. Tears are valuable. Tears have meaning. Tears speak volumes. Tears flow from the face of a person overlooked by others. Not very often can you see the tracks of someone's tears. Tears that used to stream down their face, now wiped away. They have become accustomed to hiding behind a mask. They put on a happy face and smile for the ever-present camera photo op daily, while internally, the tears still flow. Job 6:20 (NIV) says:

They are distressed, because they had been confident; they arrive there, only to be disappointed.

You shed tears from rejoicing, physical pain, emotional pain, despair, regret, frustration, depression and from death. A good, bad or ugly cry can be life changing. Change cannot manifest itself without inconvenience. Change for the good will shake, stir and mix some 'thangs' up, but when all is said and done, it will work for your good. Romans 8:28 (NASB) says:

And we know that [a]God causes all things to work together for good to those who love God, to those who are called according to His purpose.

The demons of your past will incrementally threaten your present; the past has potentially paralyzing power. But glory be to God in the highest! When you have a relationship with Him, it will provide you freedom to look forward in faith! Philippians 3:14 (NIV) says:

I press on toward the goal to win the prize for which God has called me heavenward in Christ Jesus.

You are either going into a storm; presently in a storm; or transitioning out of a storm. The turnaround is God allows you to savor the sunshine, revel in a rainbow, whisk with the wind, and ripple through a rainfall. Psalms 24:1 (NIV) says:

The earth is the Lord's, and everything in it, the world, and all who live in it;

Psalms 126:5 (NLT) says:

Those who plant in tears will harvest with shouts of joy.

Grow in your faith in God by reminding yourselves His Spirit dwells within you and He offers you His peace. Take your tears to God! Psalms 130:1 (NKJV) says:

Out of the depths I have cried to You, O Lord...

Psalms 107:6 (NASB) says:

Then they cried out to the Lord in their trouble; He delivered them out of their distresses.

Psalms 40:1 (NLT) says:

> *I waited patiently for the Lord to help me, and he turned to me and heard my cry.*

God is fully aware of your good times and your bad times. The Lord is close to you when you smile and when you are heartbroken. Metaphorically speaking, tears are prayers too; the tears make their way to God when we cannot find the right words to say to Him. Your mind needs to stay on Jesus because you love Him. He remembers you and He knows you through and through, and He records your tears. Psalms 56:8 (NLT) says:

> *You keep track of all my sorrows. You have collected all my tears in your bottle. You have recorded each one in Your book.*

Psalms 34:15 (NIV) says:

> *The eyes of the Lord are on the righteous, and his ears are attentive to their cry…*

Revelation 7:17 (NASB) says:

> *For the Lamb in the center of the throne will be their shepherd, and will guide them to springs of the [a]water of life; and God will wipe every tear from their eyes.*

You feel cornered with nowhere to run and no one to turn to; you stumble and are led astray by the sins of the world; you are unable to see your way forward due to strongholds that have you bound to past hurts, shame and degradation. You are holding onto the baggage of being overweight, divorced, abused and feeling unloved; you cannot seem to alleviate carrying these daily pains and heartache.

Be of good cheer ladies! God will not leave you hopeless! God will never leave you with a troubled heart, mind and soul. Turn it over to Him consistently and pray without ceasing! You will be able to release the poignant attacks of the enemy and move safely into the arms of our Father. Psalms 55:22 (KJV) says:

Cast thy burden upon the Lord, and he shall sustain thee: he shall never suffer the righteous to be moved.

Revelations 21:4 (NASB) says:

And He will wipe away every tear from their eyes; and there will no longer be any death; there will no longer be any mourning, or crying, or pain; the first things have passed away.

Romans 8:26-27 (NIV) says:

In the same way, the Spirit helps us in our weakness. We do not know what we ought to pray for, but the Spirit himself intercedes for us through wordless groans. And he who searches our hearts knows the mind of the Spirit, because the Spirit intercedes for God's people in accordance with the will of God.

Moment of Truth	Song
Words are Tears That Need to be Written Down. Tears are Words that need to be shed. Without Them, joy loses all its brilliance and sadness has no end. - Paulo Coelho	Changing Your Story by Jekalyn Carr Why Not Me by Tasha Page-Lockhart

PRAYER

Loving Father, thank You for a love everlasting to everlasting! Thank You for working and growing me through the rocky roads of life. Clean me up Lord! Open my heart to the needs of your children known and unknown. Continue to mold me in your image Father. Release in me those things that are not of You, Lord. Thank You for keeping me on those days I just felt overwhelmed from life's struggles. I long for your loving comfort in my time of need! Thank You for being the keeper of my tears. In Jesus' Name, Amen

Thank You

> I CHRONICLES 16:34 (NIV)
>
> Give thanks to the Lord, for He is good; His love endures forever.

Psalms 106:1 (NLT): Praise the Lord! Give thanks to the Lord, for He is good! His faithful love endures forever.

Psalms 107:1 (NLT): Give thanks to the Lord, for he is good! His faithful love endures forever.

here is a praise and worship song that simply says....

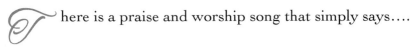 Thank You Lord, Thank You Lord, Thank You Looord; I just want to Thank You, Lord.

Cannot stop there because…

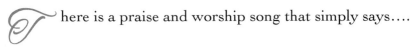 You've been so good, You've been so good, You've been so goood; I just want to Thank You, Lord.

Furthermore Lord…

🎙 You made a way, You made a way, You made a waaayyy; I just want to Thank You, Lord.

Be Thankful… God's love will last forever! James 1:17 (NIV) says:

Every good and perfect gift is from above, coming down from the Father of the heavenly lights, who does not change like shifting shadows.

For life itself, it is a gracious gift from God! Thank Him for everything He has done for you! Shout Glory to His Name! Psalms 69:30 (NASB) says:

I will praise the name of God with song and magnify Him with thanksgiving.

His glorious grace is freely given to us! Ephesians 1:16 (NASB) says:

Do not cease giving thanks for you, while making mention of you in my prayers.

God is generous and He blesses all His children equally! Ephesians 5:20 (NLT) says:

And give thanks for everything to God the Father in the name of our Lord Jesus Christ.

God does not provide material things. He gives you knowledge, hope and faith! 2 Corinthians 9:15 (NKJV) says:

Thanks be to God for His indescribable gift!

Be Grateful

You can pray in season and out of season! Do not get in the habit of only praying when you want God to make a way; He will show up and show out according to His will. Make sure you pray early and daily surrounding yourselves with the protection of the Holy Spirit and dwelling in His blessed Will everyday! Philippians 4:6-7 (MSG) says:

Don't fret or worry. Instead of worrying, pray. Let petitions and praises shape your worries into prayers, letting God know your concerns. Before you know it, a sense of God's wholeness, everything coming together for good, will come and settle you down. It's wonderful what happens when Christ displaces worry at the center of your life.

When spreading His teachings to others, make sure you keep God's Word in your heart. Colossians 3:15-17 (NIV) says:

[15] Let the peace of Christ rule in your hearts, since as members of one body you were called to peace. And be thankful. [16] Let the message of Christ dwell among you richly as you teach and admonish one another with all wisdom through Psalms, hymns, and songs from the Spirit, singing to God with gratitude in your hearts. [17] And whatever you do, whether in word or deed, do it all in the name of the Lord Jesus, giving thanks to God the Father through him.

Be Appreciative...

A spirit of gratitude must be nurtured, then passed down to others. Appreciate your earthly blessings, but make sure others know it all comes from God. Always remember to be grateful for the small stuff. Psalms 9:1 (NASB) says:

I will give thanks to the Lord with all my heart; I will tell of all Your wonders.

Amid adversity, trials, tribulations and obstacles, thank God for covering you from dangers seen and unseen! Revelation 11:17 (NIV) says:

We give thanks to you, Lord God Almighty, the One who is and who was, because You have taken Your great power and have begun to reign.

God is gracious and does not leave you to yourself to figure things out! God has a plan for your life! Be wise not to lose sight of the bigger picture. Recognize that every gift you desire may not be God's will for your life. No matter what, BE THANKFUL! Psalms 28:7 (NLT) says:

The Lord is my strength and shield. I trust Him with all my heart. He helps me, and my heart is filled with joy. I burst out in songs of thanksgiving.

Moment of Truth	Song
A thankful heart is a great virtue	Thankful by Mary Mary Grateful by Hezekiah Walker

PRAYER

Lord, please help me to be intentionally thankful. Help me to maintain a grateful spirit and a thankful heart. I desire to fill my heart full of praise that brings joy to the Father and glory to His name. Thank You for the work You are doing in me. I want an attitude of gratitude in all aspects of my life. I am thankful for just being able to wake up this morning! I am grateful I was able to clothe myself in my right mind! I am a living, breathing child of God today, and I am thankful! Lord, I will spread your blessing to others! In Jesus' Name, Amen

~ The End ~

- -

How was your experience? Please consider leaving a comment on my website at www.torrelwalls.com.